[*Praise*]

"In an ever-more complex world of gadgets, sensors, alerts, notifications, vibrations, data and digital interfaces society risks becoming overwhelmed with a myriad of options worthy, or not, of our attention. Designers and technologists need to consider how each decision they make about their product or service affects not only the immediate user but their ecosystem as a whole. This book makes that evidently clear and then points out how to be a more deliberate, considerate maker in the 21st century."
  JEFF GOTHELF, AUTHOR, *LEAN UX*

"Deceptively simple and straightforward, the book draws a comprehensive picture that connects the seminal work of 1990s Calm Technology pioneers Weiser and Brown to the design problems of the upcoming Internet of Things and of a world of constant human-information interactions. As generous with practical advice as it is with its theoretical foundations, Calm Technology offers a critical, user-centered reassessment of the interplay between design and technology in the age of pervasive and ubiquitous computing. Not a book that you'll leave on your bookshelf often."
  ANDREA RESMINI, SENIOR LECTURER, JÖNKÖPING UNIVERSITY

"At last, a set of design principles concerned more with supporting human beings than business plans. Imagine a world where technology doesn't interrupt, cajole, and agitate, but rather creates time and space for people to reflect, engage, and even breathe. Amber Case not only envisions such a reality, but has shared the way we get there."
**DOUGLAS RUSHKOFF, AUTHOR, *PRESENT SHOCK*
& *THROWING ROCKS AT THE GOOGLE BUS***

"In Calm Technology, Amber gives us ready to use patterns for designing calm interactions, as well as the underlying principles behind them. Anyone who builds things with a computer in it (which is everything) should read this book."
JOSH MARINACCI, TECHNICAL MARKETING MANAGER, PUBNUB

"In an era where we are surrounded by always-on devices, blinking, beeping, vibrating, and jostling for our attention, Amber Case's tightly focused monograph on the tenets of calm design comes at just the right time. As we rely more and more on our technology for ordinary daily life, designers, product managers, and entrepreneurs will do well to pay close attention on how our designs are affecting the mood and well being of our customers, and to learn how to design experiences that calm and soothe, instead of agitating and upsetting."
**CHRISTIAN CRUMLISH, VP PRODUCT, 7CUPS.COM & COAUTHOR,
DESIGNING SOCIAL INTERFACES, SECOND EDITION**

"I loved this book. Too often our product discussions are technology-led, but this book builds from the human out, starting off with insightful guidelines, moving into specific design patterns, and even having exercises to bring the points home. This book creates a new vocabulary we will be using in future product design."
SCOTT JENSON, PRODUCT STRATEGY, GOOGLE

Calm Technology

Principles and Patterns for Non-Intrusive Design

Amber Case

 Beijing · Boston · Farnham · Sebastopol · Tokyo

Calm Technology
by Amber Case

Copyright © 2016 Amber Case. All rights reserved.

Printed in the United States of America.

Published by O'Reilly Media, Inc., 1005 Gravenstein Highway North, Sebastopol, CA 95472.

O'Reilly books may be purchased for educational, business, or sales promotional use. Online editions are also available for most titles (*safaribooksonline.com*). For more information, contact our corporate/institutional sales department: (800) 998-9938 or *corporate@oreilly.com*.

Acquisitions Editor: Mary Treseler
Editor: Angela Rufino
Production Editor: Colleen Lobner
Copyeditor: Jasmine Kwityn
Proofreader: Rachel Head

Indexer: Lucie Haskins
Cover Designer: Randy Comer
Interior Designers: Ron Bilodeau and Monica Kamsvaag
Illustrator: Amber Case
Compositor: Colleen Lobner

December 2015: First Edition.

Revision History for the First Edition:

> 2015-12-08　　First release
> 2016-02-22　　Second release

See *http://oreilly.com/catalog/errata.csp?isbn=0636920039747* for release details.

The O'Reilly logo is a registered trademark of O'Reilly Media, Inc. *Calm Technology* and related trade dress are trademarks of O'Reilly Media, Inc.

Many of the designations used by manufacturers and sellers to distinguish their products are claimed as trademarks. Where those designations appear in this book, and O'Reilly Media, Inc., was aware of a trademark claim, the designations have been printed in caps or initial caps.

Although the publisher and author have used reasonable care in preparing this book, the information it contains is distributed "as is" and without warranties of any kind. This book is not intended as legal or financial advice, and not all of the recommendations may be suitable for your situation. Professional legal and financial advisors should be consulted, as needed. Neither the publisher nor the author shall be liable for any costs, expenses, or damages resulting from use of or reliance on the information contained in this book.

978-1-491-92588-1

[LSI]

[contents]

Preface vii

Chapter 1 **Designing for the Next 50 Billion Devices** 1
    Four Waves of Computing............................ 1
    The Next 50 Billion Devices 6
    The Future of Technology 13
    Conclusions 14

Chapter 2 **Principles of Calm Technology** 15
    The Limited Bandwidth of Our Attention 15
    Principles of Calm Technology 17
    Conclusions 51

Chapter 3 **Calm Communication Patterns** 53
    Status Indicators 54
    Ambient Awareness 68
    Contextual Notifications 73
    Persuasive Technology 78
    Conclusions 82

Chapter 4 **Exercises in Calm Technology** 85
    A Calm Interaction Evaluation Tool 86
    Exercises 90
    Conclusions 99

Chapter 5	**Calm Technology in Your Organization** **101**	
	Building Teams for Calm Technology................101	
	Design for Privacy....................................105	
	Selling Calm Technology to Managers 108	
	Entering a Product into Human Society: A Calm Product Launch 112	
	Conclusions 118	
Chapter 6	**The History and Future of Calm Technology**.........**119**	
	Videoconferencing Before Skype.....................120	
	The Beginnings of Calm Technology 121	
	Index..127	

[*Preface*]

I FIRST CAME ACROSS Mark Weiser and John Seely Brown's work "Designing Calm Technology" in 2005. I was a sophomore in college at the time, and although technology was a passion of mine, my coursework and research were primarily in anthropology—I didn't yet know how tightly linked the two disciplines actually were. I was just beginning to discover how important an understanding of human behavior was to the design of technology, and specifically, the ways we communicate with our devices.

In 2005, smartphones were just entering the landscape, transforming the humble mobile phone from a glorified walkie-talkie into a fully functioning computer that would take all of the challenges of computer user interfaces and amplify them in our daily lives. It was this research that led me to eventually write my thesis on smartphones and their impact on human culture. During my research I stumbled upon a little-known but breakthrough paper in human–computer interaction from the mid-'90s called "Designing Calm Technology." It turned out that researchers at Xerox PARC, including technologists and anthropologists from a variety of backgrounds, had been working for years on understanding the impact of technology on people's behavior and well-being.

Their chief concern was how to best design technologies for a future saturated with small devices. I realized that the subject of Calm Technology and the research underlying it were not just about where the Internet was headed, but where our entire society was headed. The topic was worth a lot more attention that it had originally received.

FIGURE P-1

Xerox PARC Computer Science Laboratory (CSL), circa 1980s, where early Internet pioneer and Lab Director Bob Taylor held informal meetings with laboratory students in beanbag chairs.*

Weiser and Brown were at least a decade ahead of their time. They were so far ahead that their work is in danger of being forgotten…precisely at the time we most need it. Weiser was the intellectual father of Ubiquitous Computing. He and Brown first introduced the concept of "Calm Technology" in their 1995 paper, published at Xerox PARC. This is still the term most commonly used to describe it, though it might be more accurate to call it "Calm Interaction," or simply "Calm Design."

We need their conceptual framework, their advice, and their research now more than ever, or we will increasingly run into issues like loss of human agency, security, and privacy, not to mention a crisis of bandwidth. None of us wants a future where we continuously update settings for apps we never use, nor do we want to always be on pause

---

* Image courtesy of PARC Research, photo credit Xerox PARC; used with permission.

while waiting for a bit of technology to fix itself. Weiser said that we wouldn't be able to interact with future technology the same way that we interact with a desktop computer. That future is now.

In 2005 we were just beginning to see the promise of mobile devices, but back in the '80s and '90s, Weiser and Brown envisioned a future full of devices much like our current televisions, smartphones, and tablets: a series of what they called "pads, tabs, and boards." As time progressed, I realized just how core their insights would be in a world increasingly mediated by technology.

My study of cell phones, social cues, and interface design quickly grew into a career in user experience (UX) and interaction design. I eventually realized that most technology gets in the way of people's lives instead of working with them. We're stuck with heavy applications struggling to work on connected smartphones with minimal battery life. How will a coming era of small devices solve this problem? We're poised to become even more anxious and overwhelmed, with everything beeping at us.

The next decade will nurture a new generation of new connected devices fraught with frustration and complexity. Many people speak of an exciting new future of devices, but we haven't solved the problems in technology we have right now. The promise of the Internet of Things (IoT) is a fallacy if it is unconnected to helping people solve problems. It's not just a fun thing you can run in your house—it *must* provide a use. Successful technology for the Internet of Things era will have to become very simple, with minimal interfaces. It is my belief that the future of the Internet of Things will be driven by "Calm Technology": elegant, humane, and unobtrusive.

This book offers some principles for developing the next generation of devices. We need new tools and a new vision to make the Internet of Things work for us, not against us. Surprisingly, that vision comes to us from a team that envisaged the future decades ago. I wrote *Calm Technology* to bring their concepts to light in the current era, so we might learn from them and not unnecessarily repeat their intellectual labor.

I will also *expand on* Weiser and Brown's ideas by reflecting on what is currently happening in the industry. The advantage of our historical perspective is that we can make observations about how technology actually developed in order to test-drive the ideas put forward by these thinkers. Smartphones, modern Internet access, and cheap sensors were only theories in their time, but they still built prototypes of what a future world would look like with them.

We can learn a lot from the conceptual framework of these thinkers by studying how they approached a future world decades before it came to be. In a sense, they were not blinded by what *was*, so they were able to clearly imagine what *could be*. They were able to think about the long-term effects of technology in an environment outside of time.

The idea of an unobtrusive technology is not new. It was a century ago that people were thinking about how to harness and create something that would become the first Calm Technology: *electricity*. Electricity is all around us. It works in the background without actively requiring our attention.

An ideal app or technology is one that becomes invisible in its functioning. It provides us a utility that we need without drawing excessive attention to itself. Unlike electricity, much of our current technology breaks without warning, or interrupts us with status or software updates, taking us out of our flow and away from our goals. It stands against us and outside of us.

Though we might think of technology as cold and inhuman, it's important to remember that technology—for all its exotic idiosyncrasies—is fundamentally human. We designed it as an extension of ourselves. It is time that we smooth that relationship for the next generation.

Who Should Read This Book

You should read this book if you actively use, design, or make decisions about technology. It is especially relevant if you happen to be a user experience designer, product manager, engineer, or executive. You should *definitely* read this book if you're bothered by poorly designed information systems and want to make them better.

This book is a look at designing for the next 50 billion devices. It asks several questions that aren't asked often enough yet, but will soon be on everyone's mind: How can we create technologies that will only demand our attention when *absolutely* necessary? How do we design for privacy, bandwidth constraints, and battery life? How can we enter products smoothly into the market and give them intelligent design for all stages of their lifecycle? And finally, how can we design technology that people love? Technology that becomes *a part of life*, and not a distraction from it? Can we design tech for generations, not just seasons?

We will soon, we are told, have fridges that tell us when to go to the store to pick up eggs, and "smart" stickers that tell us that the bananas we bought last week aren't doing so well. But I don't need a computer to tell me that some of the food in my fridge doesn't look so good anymore, and neither do you: a banana is a beautifully evolved piece of *natural technology* that visually indicates if it's past its best. I see value in receiving an alert that I am out of milk while I am at the store, but not if it depends on technology that has been funded by investors to only work well only in optimal conditions, or on a device that requires my continual attention to keep it working effectively.

Things that break add friction to our lives; they get in the way of getting something done. We talk about "smart watches" that bug you about all of the things that are going on in your life—text messages, status updates, and emails right on your wrist.

But this kind of technology takes you out of your life. It interrupts you, often with information you don't need, because it is delivered by default.

We see systemic friction all the time: each time we upgrade a phone to a new operating system, or rent a place to live and inherit different kitchen appliances with strange new buttons. Low-friction systems, on the other hand, are those that bring us data and increased capacity in a non-annoying way. We need to make technologies that can *amplify* humanness and retain human choice.

Thank you for reading this book! I hope it will help give you a framework for thinking about the future of connected devices and how you might build or modify existing devices.

If you'd like to learn more or contribute to the community, visit *http://calmtech.com* and *@calmtechbook* or *@caseorganic* on Twitter. There is also a video workshop on Calm Technology (*http://bit.ly/calm-tech-video*) available on the O'Reilly website. In addition, the latest exercises in Calm Technology will be available at *http://calmtech.com/exercises*. If you'd like to contact me, please email *case@caseorganic.com*.

How This Book Is Organized

This book is organized into six chapters:

Chapter 1: Designing for the Next 50 Billion Devices

This chapter examines the rapid growth of devices from the 1950s to the current era of Ubiquitous Computing. What do 50 billion devices mean for human attention, bandwidth, and battery life? What risks does a social network of devices have for human agency, and how can we solve these problems with Calm Design?

Chapter 2: Principles of Calm Technology

This chapter outlines a number of guidelines for designing Calm Technology. We'll cover concepts such as the limited bandwidth of attention, compressing information into our peripheral senses, and designing technology to consume the smallest amount of our mental attention. The chapter outlines the following principles:

- Technology should require the smallest possible amount of attention.
- Technology should inform and create calm.
- Technology should make use of the periphery.
- Technology should amplify the best of technology and the best of humanity.
- Technology can communicate, but doesn't need to speak.
- Technology should work even when it fails.
- The right amount of technology is the minimum needed to solve the problem.
- Technology should respect social norms.

Chapter 3: Calm Communication Patterns

Here we'll look at examples of Calm Technology grouped by how each device captures our attention. This chapter discusses simple status indicators such as lights and sounds, then goes on to examine more complex, system-based patterns such as persuasive loops and contextual notifications. These are some of the topics we'll discuss:

- Visual status indicators
- Status tones
- Haptic alerts
- Status shouts
- Ambient awareness
- Contextual notifications
- Persuasive technology

Chapter 4: Exercises in Calm Technology

This chapter gives you the opportunity to apply what you've learned in a series of exercises involving the design of common human objects.

Here's a full list of the exercises we will look at:

- Exercise 1: A Calmer Alarm Clock
- Exercise 2: A Clock That Starts the Day
- Exercise 3: A Year-Long Battery
- Exercise 4: A Calmer Kitchen
- Exercise 5: A Fridge for Healthier Eating
- Exercise 6: Using Ambient Awareness
- Exercise 7: Bringing Haptics into Play

Chapter 5: Calm Technology in Your Organization

This chapter discusses how you can integrate concepts of Calm Technology within an organization, including considerations of privacy and security. We'll cover strategies for avoiding failed launches, how to form and test teams, and how to successfully transition products into everyday life.

Chapter 6: The History and Future of Calm Technology

This final chapter more closely examines the origins of Calm Technology and Ubiquitous Computing at Xerox PARC. We'll cover some of the philosophy of the researchers at Xerox PARC and how their early work contributed to their worldview.

Safari® Books Online

Safari Books Online (*http://www.safaribooksonline.com*) is an on-demand digital library that delivers expert content in both book and video form from the world's leading authors in technology and business. Technology professionals, software developers, web designers, and business and creative professionals use Safari Books Online as their primary resource for research, problem solving, learning, and certification training.

Safari Books Online offers a range of product mixes and pricing programs for organizations, government agencies, and individuals. Subscribers have access to thousands of books, training videos, and prepublication manuscripts in one fully searchable database from publishers like O'Reilly Media, Prentice Hall Professional, Addison-Wesley Professional, Microsoft Press, Sams, Que, Peachpit Press, Focal Press, Cisco Press, John Wiley & Sons, Syngress, Morgan Kaufmann, IBM Redbooks, Packt, Adobe Press, FT Press, Apress, Manning, New Riders, McGraw-Hill, Jones & Bartlett, Course Technology, and dozens more. For more information about Safari Books Online, please visit us online.

How to Contact Us

Please address comments and questions concerning this book to the publisher:

> O'Reilly Media, Inc.
> 1005 Gravenstein Highway North
> Sebastopol, CA 95472
> 800-998-9938 (in the United States or Canada)
> 707-829-0515 (international or local)
> 707-829-0104 (fax)

We have a web page for this book, where we list errata, examples, and any additional information. You can access this page at *http://bit.ly/ calm-technology*.

To comment or ask technical questions about this book, send email to *bookquestions@oreilly.com*.

For more information about our books, courses, conferences, and news, see our website at *http://www.oreilly.com*.

Find us on Facebook: *http://facebook.com/oreilly*

Follow us on Twitter: *http://twitter.com/oreillymedia*

Watch us on YouTube: *http://www.youtube.com/oreillymedia*

Acknowledgments

To Mark Weiser, Rich Gold, and John Seely Brown for their work at Xerox PARC and the inspiration for this book.

To my primary content editors, Carl Alviani and Kellyn Bardeen, for long days and nights of in-depth help, and to the fantastic and very patient Angela Rufino, Mary Treseler, and Jasmine Kwityn, my editors at O'Reilly.

To Scott Jenson, Christian Crumlish, Adam Duvander, Marshall Kirkpatrick, and Josh Marinacci for reviewing drafts and outlines of the book as it came to life.

To my mentors Sheldon Renan, Douglas Rushkoff, and Deborah Heath. And to my parents, for raising me with a sense of wonder.

[1]

Designing for the Next 50 Billion Devices

Four Waves of Computing

THE FIRST WAVE OF COMPUTING, from 1940 to about 1980, was dominated by **many people serving one computer.** This was the era of the large and limited mainframe computer. Mainframe use was largely reserved for technically proficient experts who took on the task of learning difficult, poorly designed interfaces as a source of professional pride.

The second wave, or desktop era, had **one person to one computer.** The computer increased in power, but it was still tethered into place. We saw the era of desktop publishing and the user interface replace difficult-to-use text inputs of the generation before.

The third wave, Weiser posited, would be ushered in by the Internet, with many desktops connected through widespread distributed computing. This would be the transition between the desktop era and ubiquitous computing. It would enable many smaller objects to be connected to a larger network.

This final wave, just beginning (and unevenly distributed), has **many computers serving each person**, everywhere in the world. Mark Weiser called this wave the era of **"Ubiquitous Computing,"** or **"Ubicomp."**

Weiser's idea of Ubiquitous Computing was that **devices would outnumber individuals globally by a factor of five or more.** In other words, if there's a world population of 10 billion (which Weiser considered not so far-fetched in the 21st century), then 50 billion devices globally is a conservative estimate. Obviously, the ratio will be much higher in some parts of the world than others, but even this is beginning to level off.

Some of us are still interacting with one desktop, but most of us have multiple devices in our lives, from smartphones and laptops to small tablets and Internet-connected thermostats in our homes.

What happens when we have many devices serving one person? We run up against limits in data access and bandwidth that may lead us, through necessity, into the fourth wave, an era of **Distributed Computing.** Figure 1-1 illustrates these four waves of computing.

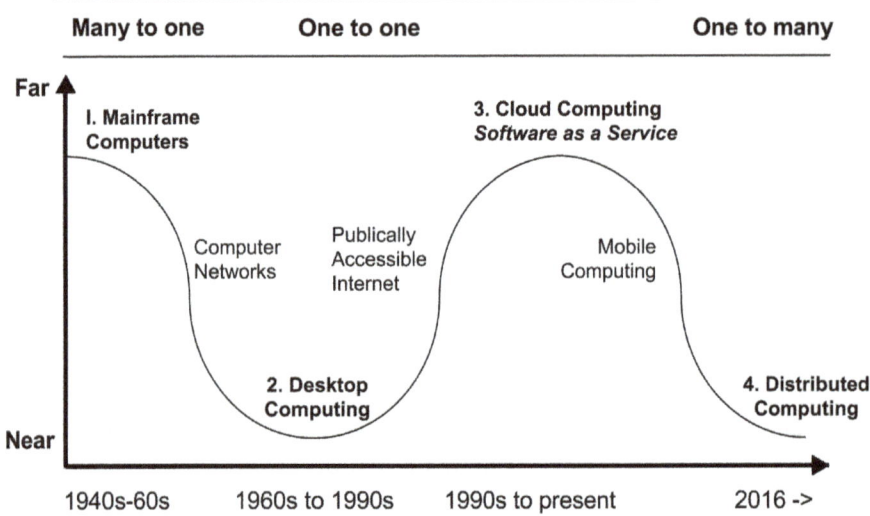

FIGURE 1-1
Waves of computing, inspired by Mark Weiser and John Seely Brown's three phases of computing in "The Coming Age of Calm Technology," Xerox PARC, 1996.

Ubiquitous Computing describes the state of affairs in which many devices in our personal landscape possess some kind of processing power but are not all necessarily connected to one another. What we know today as **the "Internet of Things" is meant to describe a network between many devices,** so represents a *networked* stage of Ubiquitous Computing; it also implies that many everyday objects, like your tennis shoes, may also become wirelessly connected to the network, opening up a whole range of new functionality, data collection possibilities, and security risks. Although it might be great to be able to track your daily steps, it might not be as nice if that data falls into the wrong hands. **In Distributed Computing, every device on the network is used as a potential node for storing information.** This means that even if a central server is taken out, it is still possible to access a file or piece of information normally hosted by the central server, because these bytes of information are "distributed" throughout the network.

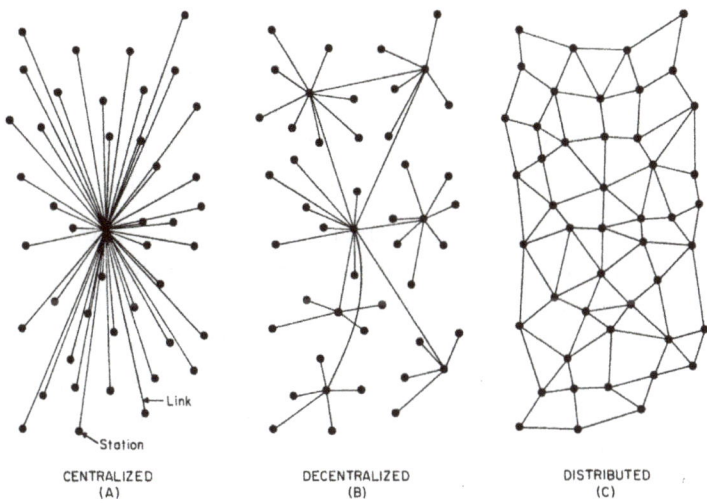

FIGURE 1-2
Centralized, decentralized, and distributed systems.*

Weiser's original vision for Ubicomp also included a philosophy about how to handle the increase in devices per person. What happens when 50 billion devices are out there? In a world like this, **the way devices communicate with us is crucial.** If we were to expand their number but maintain our current standards of communication, we'd soon find ourselves—our entire world—buried under an indistinguishable pile of dialog boxes, pop-up boxes, push notifications, and alarms.

---

* Source: Paul Baran, "On Distributed Communications," Rand Corporation, 1964. *http://www.rand.org/content/dam/rand/pubs/research_memoranda/2006/RM3420.pdf.*

THE WORLD IS NOT A DESKTOP

Gone are the luxurious dinosaurs of the desktop era, where code could be the size of a CD-ROM and be updated every two years. The act of using a desktop computer is an all-consuming process—a luxury that not all current devices share.

Desktop applications were able to take advantage of many resources in terms of processing power, bandwidth, and attention. A desktop computer assumes that you will sit in front of it in a chair, rooted to place, with all of your attention on a single screen. A mobile device, on the other hand, may be competing with your environment for attention. Rarely will you be sitting down in front of it. Instead, you might be outside or in a restaurant, in a state of focus that technologist Linda Stone calls "continuous partial attention." A smaller, connected device today may work on tiny processors and need to make use of what it has.

Small devices must be cheap in order to be ubiquitous. They must be fast in order to be used. They must be capable of easily connecting if they are to survive. We're looking more at a whole new species than we are a mechanical set of items. That means nature's laws apply. Fast, small, and quickly reproducing devices will end up being part of the next generation, but **good design can make products that span multiple generations**, reducing complexity and the need for support.

We're moving toward an ecosystem that is more organic than it is mechanical. We have computer viruses that operate similarly to their counterparts in nature. In this new era, code bloat is not only unnecessary—it is dangerous. To follow this analogy, a poorly written system invites illness and decay.

THE GROWING EPHEMERALITY OF HARDWARE

In the desktop era, hardware was stable. You bought a computer and kept it for several years—the hardware itself was an investment. You'd change or update the software very infrequently. It would come on a CD-ROM or packaged with the computer. Now, people hold on to the data streams and the software longer than the devices themselves. How many different phones has the average person used to connect to their profile on Facebook? Facebook, despite comprising dozens of rapidly shifting apps and programs, is more stable as a whole than the technology on which it is used.

No longer do people buy devices to use for a decade; now, technology may be upgraded within a single year. Companies and carriers are now offering monthly payment plans that allow you to be automatically "subscribed" to the latest device, eliminating the process of buying each device as it comes out. It's an investment in the *functionality* and the *data*, not the device itself. **It's more about the data than the technology that serves it; the technology is just there to serve the data to the user.**

In the past, technology's primary value lay in hardware. Now a greater value lies in user-generated content. This means the simplest technology to get to that data wins; it's easier to use, develop, support, and maintain.

THE SOCIAL NETWORK OF 50 BILLION THINGS

In the future, connected *things* will far outnumber connected *people*.

Consider a social network of 50 billion devices versus a social network of 10 billion humans. **The social network of objects won't just be about alerts for humans via machines, but alerts from one machine to another.**

With so many objects and systems, one of the most important issues will be how those separate networks communicate with one another. This can lead to some real problems. Have you ever been stuck in a parking garage because the ticket machine won't accept your money? When an entire system is automated with no human oversight, it can get stuck in a loop. What if a notification gets stuck in one system and can't be read by another? What if a transaction drops entirely? Will there be notifications that the system failed, or will humans be put on pause while a human operator intervenes?

Technology in the real world can't work well all of the time. In reality, things mess up when you need them most—like when you can't get to the AAA app when your car is stuck on the side of the road, or when you can't access your insurance card when you get to the emergency room because your phone is dead or your card is at home, and your life is at risk.

The Next 50 Billion Devices

Tech can't take up too many resources in the future. The most efficient tech will eventually begin to win out, as resources, time, attention, and support become scarce commodities. People will have to make less complex systems or suffer the consequences.

Though technology might not have a limit, we do. Our environment also has limited connectivity and power. Things are going to become much more expensive over time.

The IDC FutureScape: Worldwide Internet of Things (IoT) 2015 Predictions report[†] suggests that "IT networks are expected to go from having excess capacity to being overloaded by the stress of Internet of Things (IoT) connected devices" in just three years.

This means that devices using too much bandwidth will experience connectivity and performance issues, and generate unnecessary costs. Overcoming this bandwidth limitation will take a combination of solutions, all of which need to happen at some point. One solution is Distributed Computing, which might be a natural outcome of bandwidth and content restraints. Another solution is to limit bandwidth usage by placing limits on how large websites and content can be. We'll examine some of these solutions later in this chapter.

Where did telephone lines, the electrical grid, or modern roads come from? All of these required an invested government and business-based effort. Without them, we wouldn't have the access and connectivity we have today.

Today's telecom carriers and Internet providers build competing, redundant networks and don't share network capacity, which makes it much more difficult for devices to communicate with one another.

It is ultimately in companies' best interests to build more bandwidth as they grow, but the costs associated with this development could harm initial earnings and allow competitors a leg up while they build. Telecom and Internet providers might be forced to work differently in the future. If they worked together, they might be able to devise a way to share the costs and rewards of building infrastructure. If not,

---

† IDC FutureScape: Worldwide Internet of Things (IoT) 2015 Predictions. (*http://www.thewhir.com/web-hosting-news/half-networks-will-feel-stranglehold-iot-devices-idc-report*)

the government might need to take over this role, much like President Eisenhower's creation of the Interstate Highway System to eliminate unsafe roads and inefficient routes.

LIMIT BANDWIDTH USAGE

The websites we visit are designed to be appealing, and resource usage is considered primarily where it impacts usability. Websites that require significant bandwidth can slow down entire networks. The average smartphone user today is able to stream a variety of online media at will, over cell networks and WiFi. All of this volume and inefficiency is eating up the bandwidth that will soon be needed to connect the Internet of Things. This is already causing corporate conflict, with users caught up in the middle. In 2014, the Internet service providers Comcast and Verizon were caught throttling the traffic from video-streaming service provider Netflix. Netflix countered this limitation by paying the providers for more bandwidth, but even then, Verizon was still found to be throttling Netflix traffic.

Over time, bandwidth constraints might naturally push people to write software that uses less bandwidth. Companies that do well in the future might use technologies and protocols that rewrite the fabric of the Web, instituting protocols that eliminate redundancy in streaming data to many devices.

A *distributed* Web in which many devices also act as servers is one way the Web can evolve and scale. Instead of many devices requesting data from a single server, **devices could increasingly request chunks of data from one another.** We're seeing slow developments in this area today, and hopefully there will be many more in the future.

DEDICATE SEPARATE CHANNELS FOR DIFFERENT KINDS OF TECHNOLOGY

Connected devices could have their own connected channels. Dedicated channels could also serve as a backbone for devices to communicate in case of emergencies. That way, one network can still stay up if the other one becomes overloaded, so that millions of people streaming a popular video won't get in the way of a tsunami alert or a 911 call.

FIGURE 1-3

The first web server on the World Wide Web was a NeXT workstation (a NeXTcube) used by Tim Berners-Lee at CERN. The document resting on the keyboard is a copy of *Information Management: A Proposal*, which was Berners-Lee's original proposal for the World Wide Web.‡

USE LOWER-LEVEL LANGUAGES FOR MISSION-CRITICAL SYSTEMS

If we're going to be building truly resilient technology, we need to borrow a page from the past—where technologies were made with very low failure rates, or had enough edge cases accounted for in the design. Edge cases are unpredictable problems that arise at extremes. For instance, a running shoe might work well on typical pavement, but melt on track material on very hot summer days. Oftentimes edge cases are discovered after products are launched. In the worst circumstances, they may cause recalls. In June 2006, a Dell laptop burst into

---

‡ Photo by Coolcaesar (*https://commons.wikimedia.org/wiki/File:First_Web_Server.jpg*) (GFDL (*http://www.gnu.org/copyleft/fdl.html*) or CC-BY-SA-3.0 (*http://creativecommons.org/licenses/by-sa/3.0*)), via Wikimedia Commons.

flames[§] during a technical conference in Japan. The issue was a defective battery prone to overheating. This prompted a worldwide recall of laptops that contained the battery, but not before six other people reported flaming machines. Edge cases are a fact of life for all products. They might be difficult to predict, but there are some ways to lessen the blow. If possible, involve industry veterans in your project and have them help think through various edge cases and ways that the software or hardware could go wrong. Chances are, they've seen it all before. With their help, a crisis or uncomfortable situation could be prevented.

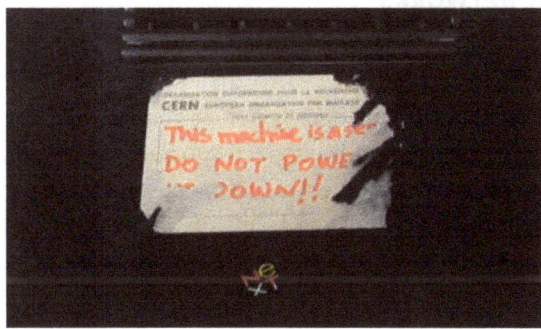

FIGURE 1-4
The partially peeled off label on the NeXTcube reads: "This machine is a server. DO NOT POWER IT DOWN!!" If this computer was turned off during the early days (when this was the lone web server), it would take down everything available on the Web.[¶]

If we're making devices that absolutely need to work, then we can't use the same development methods we've become accustomed to today. We need to go back to older, more reliable methods of building systems that do not fail.

COBOL was the first widely used high-level programming language for business applications. Although many people consider the language to be old news today, it is worth noting that:

[§] "Dell Laptop Explodes in Flames," 2006. (*http://gizmodo.com/182257/dell-laptop-explodes-in-flames*)

[¶] Credit: Ibid.

70–75% of the business and transaction systems around the world run on COBOL. This includes credit card systems, ATMs, ticket purchasing, retail/POS systems, banking, payroll systems, telephone/cell calls, grocery stores, hospital systems, government systems, airline systems, insurance systems, automotive systems, and traffic signal systems. 90% of global financial transactions are processed in COBOL.**

COBOL may be complex to write, but the systems that use it run most of the time.

CREATE MORE LOCAL NETWORKS

Today, it is only slightly inconvenient if websites like Twitter go down or become overloaded. What's less cute is when the lock on your door stops working because your phone's battery is flat, or your electric car only works some of the time because it is connected to a remote power grid. The preceding advice is especially crucial for people and agencies building websites—**the real world is not a website.**

Do we really want the lights in our homes to connect to the cloud before they can turn on or off? In the case of a server failure, do we want to be stuck without light? No, we want the light switch to be immediate. A light switch is best connected to a local network, or an analog network. It's OK for a website to go down, but not the lights in your house.

We need to prioritize the creation of a class of devices that do things locally, then go to the network to upload statistics or other information. Not all technology needs to operate in this fashion, but **the physical technology that we live with and rely on daily *must* be resilient enough that it can work regardless of whether or not it is connected to a network.**

DISTRIBUTED AND INDIVIDUAL COMPUTING

Increasingly, our computing happens elsewhere. We make use of data on the cloud that's far away from us, all the while having perfectly advanced computers in our pockets. There are loads of privacy and security issues with so much data going up and down to the cloud. A

** "Is there still a market for Cobol skills/developers?" report by Henry Ford College Computer Information Systems, 2009. *https://cis.hfcc.edu/faq/cobol*.

December 2014 report on the future of the Internet of Things[††] made a prediction that within five years, over 90% of IoT-generated data would be hosted in the cloud. Although this might make the access to data and the interaction among various connected devices easier, "cloud-based data storage will also increase the chance of cyber attacks with 90 percent of IT networks experiencing breaches related to IoT." The amount of data generated by the devices will make it a tempting target.

As an illustration of this point, in 2014, the iCloud photo storage accounts of 100 celebrities were hacked and nude photos of several A-list celebrities were leaked onto the Web. One way to reduce the insecurity of cloud-based data storage is to have devices run on private local networks. Doing so will prevent hackers from hacking all of the data from the cloud at once, even if some opportunity is lost in connecting to larger networks in real time.

The best products and services in the future will make use of local networks and personal resources. For instance, if sensitive data is stored on shared servers in the cloud, there are privacy and security issues. Sensitive data is better stored close to the person, on a personal device with boundaries for sharing (and protections preventing that private data from being searched without a warrant), and backed up on another local device such as a desktop computer or hard drive. Individual computing will help keep personal data where it is safe instead of remotely stored in a place where it can be compromised. Storing data on your personal devices will also speed up interaction time. Your applications will only go to the network if they absolutely need to.

In the era of Distributed Computing, there will also be more options for where data is stored. Table 1-1 lists several data types and provides suggestions for the best places for each type to be stored. It also shows the potential consequences in case the security of this data is compromised.

[††] "Half of IT Networks Will Feel the Stranglehold of IoT Devices: IDC Report," 2014. (*http://www.thewhir.com/web-hosting-news/half-networks-will-feel-stranglehold-iot-devices-idc-report*)

TABLE 1-1. Suggestions for how to store various data types, and potential consequences of security failure

DATA TYPE	BEST LOCATION FOR DATA	CONSEQUENCES IF DATA IS LOST, OR THE NETWORK IS COMPROMISED OR DISRUPTED
Sensitive/personal data	On a personal device such as a phone, laptop, backup hard drive, or home computer	Loss of employment; public humiliation; bullying or social isolation, which could potentially lead to suicide
Medical data	On a local device that can be shared with medical professionals on a timed clock ("Share your data with this system for this purpose for a specific period of time"; afterward, the data is deleted and the system sanitized)	Blackmailing; loss of employment
Business data (e.g., LinkedIn profile)	On publicly accessible servers (shared)	N/A (this data was created with the intention of sharing it)
Home automation system	On a local network within the home without access to a larger network	Loss of access to or control of lights, thermostats, or other home systems

INTEROPERABILITY

One of the biggest technology issues in the future is going to come from systems that don't talk to one another. Without connectivity throughout different networks, people can get caught in very difficult situations.

I rented a car once for a conference in Denver, Colorado. Initially it seemed fine, but once I got it onto the highway, the car wouldn't go above 30 miles per hour.

I pulled into a parking lot and called emergency roadside assistance. Instead of being instantly connected to an emergency line, I was put on hold for 22 minutes. I was told to leave the car in the lot and that a tow truck would come pick it up. I was going to be late for my meeting, so I called a cab and headed into town. I figured I'd cancel my entire rental car reservation for the trip.

On the 50-minute cab ride to the hotel, I called the rental company to cancel the car reservation. I was put through to four different people, connected by a support person to two discontinued support numbers, and had to identify myself and explain my situation every time. They wondered where the car was. I told them emergency roadside assistance had picked it up. They didn't have confirmation of the pickup or who I was.

I finally got them to cancel the rental, and I asked for a confirmation code. Three days later, I got the charge for the full rental. I had to get my employers to call a special number to reverse the charge and explain the situation. I was stuck in an automation trap. The systems didn't talk to each other.

How can one product inform another? What can be done to keep different systems, or at least the people who are manning them, informed the entire way through a process? The real world runs on interconnected systems, not separate ones. Without ways for systems to communicate, you can get completely stuck.

HUMAN BACKUP

Without feedback, people won't be able to tell what's going on with a system. They might assume something is happening when it isn't, or get frustrated or stuck as automation increases. For critical systems, always ensure people are around in case something breaks, and make sure there are systems that pass information from one system to another in human-readable fashion!

The Future of Technology

Poorly made products are everywhere, waiting for innovation.

We are accustomed to buying products as they come out, in seasons. People are advised not to buy an Apple product halfway through a lifecycle, but to wait for the next one. We discard the old for the new. And it makes sense: devices quickly become incompatible with current hardware and software. The last few generations of devices are unusable, toxic garbage that gets shipped off to the landfill.

The past was about having very few high-quality products in the home. Already we're finding people moving from the suburbs to walkable communities in the city. The question is: can we improve the future in time to prevent the worst outcomes in terms of pollution, a growing population, and a warming climate, or are we going to be too late?

Want to make great products? Improve the mundane! A high-quality product can keep you employed for the rest of your life, and your community, too. So many of us are caught up in designing something "new" that we forget that we can simply improve what's already around us. All of those things you don't like in your everyday life, but put up with? Ripe for innovation! Design them in a way that lasts for more than a couple of years and you will be on your way to a successful and beloved product with passionate users.

Conclusions

In this chapter, we covered the four waves of computing and what that means for the future of connected devices. We also covered how in the near future technology will run into issues such as bandwidth and design limitations, and some possible outcomes for technology and humanity.

Weiser and Brown hinted at a number of guidelines in their published work. In the following chapter, we'll take these guidelines and put them into an organized philosophy of designing Calm Technology.

These are the key takeaways from this chapter:

- We've gone from many people to one computer, to many computers per person. The next wave of computing will make demands on us in terms of privacy, security, bandwidth, and attention.

- We can no longer design technology in the way we designed for desktops. We need to think about how we'll design for the next 50 billion devices. We can help make the future more reasonable by writing efficient code, using lower-level languages for mission-critical systems, and creating more local networks. Consider distributed and individual computing, and design with interoperability in mind.

[2]

Principles of Calm Technology

The most profound technologies are those that disappear. They weave themselves into the fabric of everyday life until they are indistinguishable from it.

Consider writing, perhaps the first information technology... Not only do books, magazines and newspapers convey written information, but so do street signs, billboards, shop signs and even graffiti. Candy wrappers are covered in writing.

The constant background presence of these products of "literacy technology" does not require active attention, but the information to be conveyed is ready for use at a glance.

...we are trying to conceive a new way of thinking about computers in the world, one that takes into account the natural human environment and allows the computers themselves to vanish into the background.
  MARK WEISER, "THE COMPUTER FOR THE 21ST CENTURY"

The Limited Bandwidth of Our Attention

THIS CHAPTER WILL COVER the principles of designing Calm Technology and how they can work to conserve and respect human attention. If there's one fundamental truth that demands a new approach to technology, it's this: although the number of alerts vying for our attention has increased, the amount of attention we have remains the same. Imagine if interacting with writing, Mark Weiser's example of an ideal information technology, required as much active attention as our current technology requires.

Today we face overwhelming information in almost every aspect of our lives. No longer is data something we examine at work—it is part of our homes and our cars, and a constant resident in our purses and pockets. Our social lives, our houses and TV sets, laptops and phones are bombarding us with data constantly.

They are always drawing more attention from us, but our attention is already overdrawn by the devices we have. The reality is this: **we are not bad at technology, technology is bad at us.** This book is about *improving* the relationship between humans and technology, saving thousands of hours of development, countless design revisions, and millions of dollars in product loss. This book is meant as a reference for designing objects, both physical and virtual. We need our devices to *disappear* into our environment more, allowing us to conduct our lives with less technological friction.

This means we need to design toward minimalism and simplicity: the *minimum amount of tech* means the *minimum amount of support*. This doesn't mean the minimum amount of development time! It means instead that the designers went through enough edge cases and "everyday situations" to determine what could go wrong *before* delivering the products to market, and designed solutions into those products before the initial launch.

If **good design** allows someone to get to their goal with the *fewest steps*, Calm Technology allows them to get there with the **lowest mental cost**. These principles are guidelines to consider when designing technology:

> I. Technology should require the smallest possible amount of attention.
>
> II. Technology should inform and create calm.
>
> III. Technology should make use of the periphery.
>
> IV. Technology should amplify the best of technology and the best of humanity.
>
> V. Technology can communicate, but doesn't need to speak.
>
> VI. Technology should work even when it fails.

VII. The right amount of technology is the minimum needed to solve the problem.

VIII. Technology should respect social norms.

In this chapter, we will lay out the principles of design in an abstract way; later chapters will go into more of their application in designing technology. We need to learn how to design for the long term, which means writing code that is small instead of large. It means **valuing simple systems over complex ones**. It means designing technology for generations, not just seasons.

Principles of Calm Technology

The principles of Calm Technology are not hard-and-fast rules. You might find that some principles are more applicable to the specific product or service you are building, and that others are not applicable at all—a fire alarm system, for example, should command your full attention (when it's alerting you to an actual fire, anyway). **Not every tech project needs all eight**; principles I through IV might not come into play, while principles V through VIII do. But as we move into a future crowded with new environments and edge cases, with unpredictable connectivity, more and more categories of product are going to benefit from these principles. And keeping these ideas in mind when making early design decisions could well reduce usability issues you encounter when products first launch.

I. TECHNOLOGY SHOULD REQUIRE THE SMALLEST POSSIBLE AMOUNT OF ATTENTION

As we've already discussed, attention overload is now the single biggest bottleneck most technologies face, and the strongest argument for making technology "calm." The more things you have to pay attention to, the less mental space you have available for actually getting things done, and the more stressful those interactions are going to be.

Ideally, technology should allow us to shift our attention to it very briefly, get the information we need, and shift back, letting us attend to more things in our environment without being overwhelmed. **When building technology, we should strive to communicate information to the user without interrupting** or distracting them from their primary goal.

When you sit down in front of a workstation, your primary focus is on the machine in front of you, and nothing else. And while this works well for the increasingly narrow slice of technological interaction that is strictly productivity-minded, it's a terrible paradigm for the **massively parallel, mobile, multiplatform environment** that most of us inhabit today.

Today we have enough mobile technology making demands on our attention that it is *literally impossible* to interact with everything as if it were a desktop device. And it's not necessary: the fact is that most of what we use technology *for* doesn't explicitly require our full attention, and if it does, it doesn't require it for long. Sitting down, booting up a machine, loading a mail program and clicking on your inbox just to see if anyone sent you a note made sense in 1999, but today it makes about as much sense as sitting someone down in a dedicated conversation room just so you can say "hi."

Attention is still not a widespread consideration in design, because it wasn't nearly as crucial an issue in the desktop computing era that defined so much of what we know about human–computer interaction. Most technology right now is still designed like a desktop machine, to some degree. It forces you to focus all of your attention on it in order to receive any useful information. Unlike an oven or a teapot, it makes use of visual feedback on screens instead of tones or other audio-based alerts, making it difficult to do other things at the same time. We take for granted that you can set an oven to preheat and then walk away, but imagine if you had to stare at it the entire time!

A lot of our connected technology doesn't "just work" right out of the box, despite the advances we've made in recent decades. It must first be hooked up to a network or Bluetooth. It may need an update before it even starts, and then additional updates almost continually, each requiring you to break from your task or retrieve pieces of information, and often changing the user interface without your permission or knowledge, forcing you to relearn the application all over again.

The power cord for a MacBook doesn't need an interface to tell you when it is charging; you can open the laptop and see the indicator on the screen, but the charging indicator is built right into the cord (see Figure 2-1). In this case, **the visual display is the secondary information system of the product** (the primary one is the light indicator). You can get more information from the display, but the single most relevant and useful piece of information is available at a glance. **Consider doing away with an interface or screen entirely, replacing it with physical buttons or lights.**

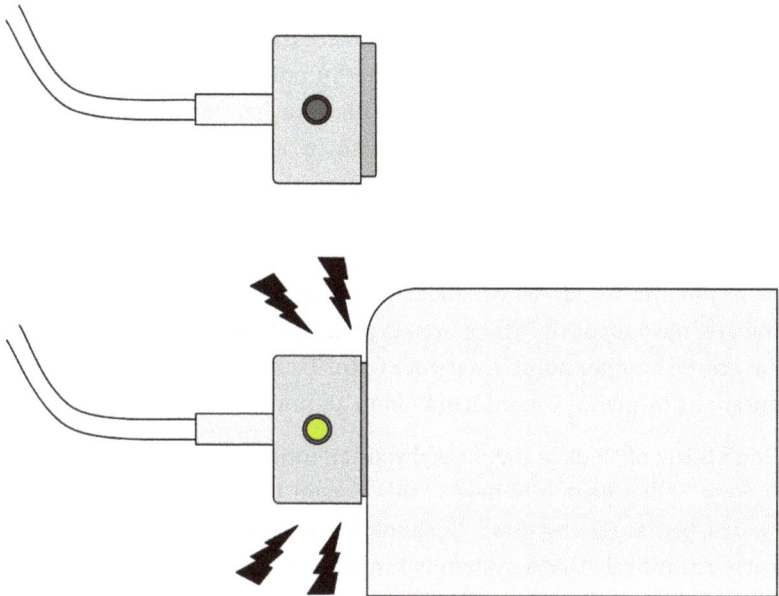

FIGURE 2-1

The indicator light on the MacBook power cord turns green when the computer is connected to a power source; it turns orange when the laptop is charging.

A video camera utilizes a very small light to show whether the camera is recording or not. The light is off by default, but when it's on, it tells both the user and the subject that recording is taking place. Google Glass didn't have one of these indicator lights for recording, leading people to be unnerved by the tech. When it's uncertain whether something is operating—especially if it's recording information—people tend to assume that it is.

Light is not the only alert style you might use. We'll get into a complete catalog of indicator types in the next chapter, but think about audio. Sometimes it's more informative to use a buzz as an alert, or a calm tone. Consider the environment in which the technology is likely to be used. Is it noisy? Crowded? Will the user be constrained from looking at the device? Think about using vibration when the user needs an indicator, but nobody else does. They'll be likely to feel the vibrating device, even if the environment is noisy.

Conversely, will the device be used in a calm, quiet environment? Use a calm tone to indicate status without unnecessary disruption, but at the same time, take advantage of the quiet in order to carry the message across. This kind of alert works well on a washer or dryer in a home: loud enough to be heard unambiguously in other rooms in the house, but not shrill enough to disturb the peace.

II. TECHNOLOGY SHOULD INFORM AND CREATE CALM

Have you ever wondered whether something was done or not? How far you are into a road trip? If the oven is preheated or not? Whether a team has scored another point in a game? Calm Technology can answer such questions by giving you information in an unobtrusive way.

Don't think of "look at me, I need your attention," but rather "this task is done," "this person is here," "this person is on their way," or even "your Uber is arriving now." Technology can create calm by letting you know definitively that a system is functioning correctly and all is well. The calm comes from knowing that you will be alerted at the appropriate time if something needs to be addressed.

The Uber example is especially useful, because it cuts down on the uncertainty of when the Uber is going to get there. You call, put the phone in your pocket, and forget about it; the app buzzes when the car is approaching. In a similar way, the "your package has arrived" message from Amazon is helpful for letting you know it's time to go home and pick it up, or that you should look out for it when you get home, or simply to open the front door.

In fact, most **information that comes from devices can be presented in a calm way.** This is just a matter of good design. Don't believe me? Think how much free-floating anxiety you could avoid with a simple system that accurately indicates that your whole complex system is running just fine, so you actually don't need to worry about it until it tells you it needs attention.

Think of how many things in your life just happen without you noticing: water when you turn on the faucet, the lights when you flip a switch, the realization that a friend is online given by a green indicator in Skype or Google Chat (Figure 2-2). All of these are technologies that are calm because they have evolved to work with us in our everyday lives with the least amount of friction.

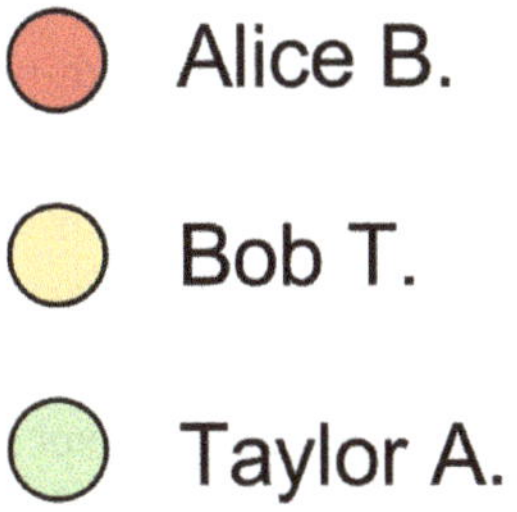

🔴 Alice B.

🟡 Bob T.

🟢 Taylor A.

FIGURE 2-2
Status indicators for available, away from computer, and offline on an online messaging system.

A shrill alert yanks you out of your current task and requires you to refocus attention on something new. Sometimes experiences should be uncalm and unnerving, like a fire alarm or a tornado warning. These are designed specifically to change your tempo—they interrupt so that you can get out of the building. **They interrupt your life for the purpose of *saving* your life.**

Before you design a notification, ask yourself *where* the person will be using the product or service. How does their environment come into play? Is the environment quiet or loud? Is it public or private?

Then you're ready to ask how the technology will communicate. Is there a way you can inform the user without distracting from their primary focus? Also ask what might happen if the primary alert fails. Can you design an alert with redundancy?

All of these considerations add to your task as a designer. But properly done, design will remove the burden of tasks from the user, which is the goal of Calm Technology.

III. TECHNOLOGY SHOULD MAKE USE OF THE PERIPHERY

A calm technology engages both the center and the periphery of our attention, and in fact moves back and forth between the two.
   MARK WEISER AND JOHN SEELY BROWN, "THE COMING AGE OF CALM TECHNOLOGY"

A calm experience is when you're performing a primary task and an alert shows up in your periphery, like the dashboard light indicating you need to fill up the gas tank, or the one telling you you're too close to the side of the road. Indications like these improve or inform your primary task (in this case, driving) and give you a sense of calm while you do something else. A calm experience does not demand your full attention.

The *periphery of our attention* is important because we can't focus our attention on many different things at once. We have high-resolution perception in front of our faces, directly in line with our vision, and that resolution degrades as we move off to the sides. We can, however, hear sounds, see shapes, and feel objects without having to directly look at them. The focus directly in front of us is limited to our sight and sometimes our touch, but there are many more layers to our spectrum of perception than just sight.

The truth is most of the information we need from technology doesn't have to be high resolution to be useful. **When a technology forces a low-resolution update into the high-resolution space of your full attention, it wastes your time, attention, and patience.** This is why it's crucial, when building a piece of technology, to consider whether the update you're trying to get across is actually a high-resolution or low-resolution one. Does it require the user's whole attention, or can you get it across with a lower resolution alert type?

Driving is a prime example of this principle in action. Over many decades, we've evolved the car driver's environment into a complex, multisensory, largely peripheral interface. Honks are sound; the vehicle moving forward is something we feel, as are the pedals we use with our feet, without having to look at them.

We see lights turn red or green, or stop signs and other road signs right in front of us because they are the punctuation of traffic and require our attention. But we can still sense where cars are around us. The mirrors in the vehicle help us glance at our periphery to see cars behind and to the sides of us, allowing us to get relevant information without having to stop our primary task of watching the road and controlling the car.

Lights that tell us about the engine turn on only when relevant. They are not on all of the time. We can switch on a turn signal while driving or turn on the stereo simply by feeling for it. **Using touch, sound, and peripheral vision opens up our sight to focus entirely on the road while doing secondary tasks in our periphery.**

Compressing Information into an Indicator

You might have heard the story about the "no brown M&Ms clause" in Van Halen's touring contract. Most people thought this was an example of the band being entitled rock stars, but it was actually a brilliant way for Van Halen's technical crew to determine whether the contract had been read or not.* Van Halen often toured with semi trucks full of equipment, and sometimes smaller stages couldn't bear the load. After a few close encounters with local crews underestimating the weight of the equipment on stage and endangering the audience, lead singer David Lee Roth decided to put a gotcha in the contract. No brown M&Ms. This brilliant example of a calm technology allowed all of the variables of the show to be compressed into a single indicator. Are there brown M&Ms in the bowl? There will probably be a technical error. As the singer wrote in his autobiography: "So, when I would walk backstage, if I saw a brown M&M in that bowl...well, line-check the entire production. Guaranteed you're going to arrive at a technical error." The consequences for technical errors could be severe. "Sometimes it would threaten to just destroy the whole show. Something like, literally, life-threatening."†

---

* "Brown Out," Snopes, 2014. (*http://www.snopes.com/music/artists/vanhalen.asp*)
† Roth, David Lee. *Crazy from the Heat.* New York: Hyperion, 1997.

A vehicle, a teapot, a washer/dryer have all evolved over time to meet our needs. They work with us and we work with them in the periphery. But new devices, such as smartphones, have become part of our everyday lives but haven't yet learned to be calm or quiet. Just like the desktop computers of the '80s, they frequently demand our full attention, distract us, beep at us, and don't make use of the periphery.

A useful way to think of this is to decide whether your technology is a **primary goal or task**, or a **secondary task** during the pursuit of a primary goal.

The group messaging software known as Slack (*https://slack.com*) got its start as part of an online game called Glitch. It was originally designed not as a standalone app, but as an integrated chat interface that allowed people to communicate while playing the game. Ironically, its origin as a secondary tool may be what has made Slack so successful.

Because it was never intended to take up your full attention, it was designed from the start to work well within an environment where the user's focus is directed elsewhere.

The Slack interface dashboard communicates things like active users and unread channels through subtle cues like colored dots and text that toggles between bold and standard typeface (see Figure 2-3). When running in the background, it announces new messages via a small blue dot on its desktop icon. When it gets disconnected, it simply turns your text box yellow while reconnecting, rather than interrupting you with a pop-up box or text message.

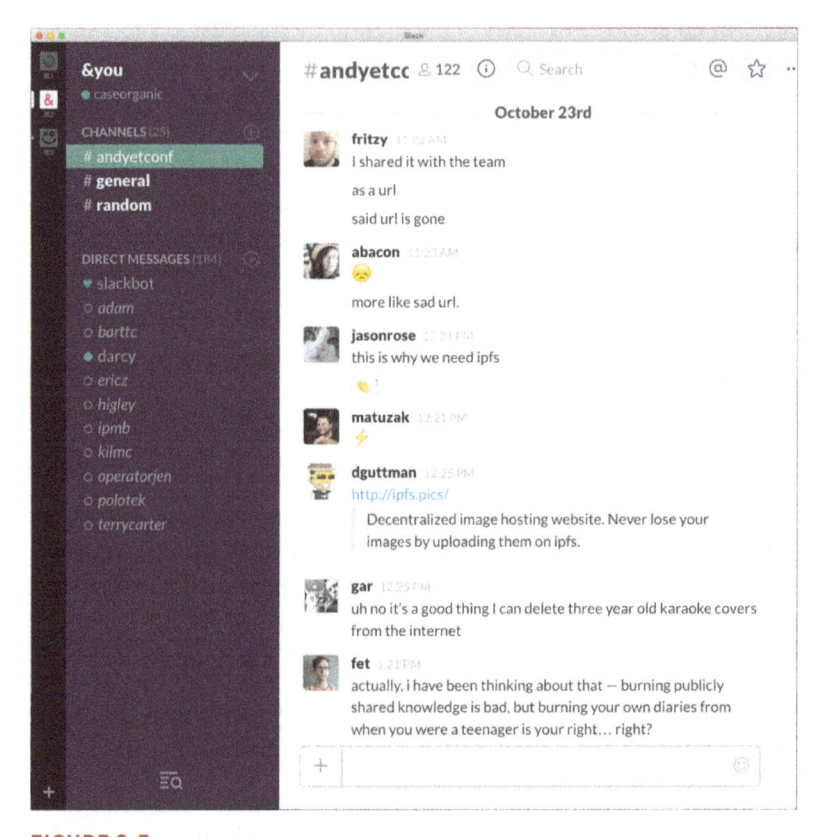

FIGURE 2-3

The Slack internal communication system.

A lot of talk in recent years about learning interaction techniques from game design focuses on features like leaderboards and reward medals. As Slack indicates, one of the great contributions of game design to productivity software has been an improved ability to get secondary tasks out of the way of the primary one, whether it's shooting goblins or writing code. In Glitch, the primary task was to play the game; communication was secondary, but necessary. An office environment is exactly the same. **The primary task should be work, and communication secondary.**

As we get more and more devices making demands on our attention, we find it more difficult to get primary tasks done. We go online to respond to an email and get distracted by a Facebook message, text message, or article.

User interface researcher Antti Oulasvirta and his Finnish collaborators created what they called the "Resource Competition Framework" to describe the results of attention disruption on completing tasks. They discussed how competing information technologies forces users to switch back and forth between tasks and external sources, temporarily leaving the switched-from tasks on hold or slowing them down.[*] For instance, a cell phone user sitting at a dinner table down the street might try to participate in the conversation of stablemates, but might find themselves frequently interrupted. A person trying to finish writing a work email might get distracted by a smartwatch alert.

Attention models

Assuming not every piece of information goes to the periphery, then, how do we prioritize? What goes where? The answer lies in **delegating primary, secondary, and tertiary attention.** Primary attention is visual and direct—namely, the attention you might pay to the road in a car, or the attention you might pay to a desktop computer. Secondary attention is more distant—the attention you pay to auditory signals or vibrations that do not need to be directly focused on in order to be felt. Tertiary consists of peripheral attention such as distant sound, light, or environmental vibration. In a vehicle, primary attention is on driving, so the windshield of the car must be the primary focus at all times. The secondary information is in the rearview mirrors and side windows, as

---

[*] Oulasvirta, Antti, Sakari Tamminen, Virpi Roto, and Jaana Kuorelahti. "Interaction in 4-second Bursts: The Fragmented Nature of Attentional Resources in Mobile HCI." *Proceedings of SIGCHI Conference on Human Factors in Computing Systems*, 2005, 919-28.

well as the feedback from the gas and brake pedals, the speedometer, and any status lights on the dashboard. The blinker function, radio, radio dial, and emergency light function all communicate tertiary information. In some cases, secondary or tertiary information might include the in-vehicle direction system.

The following tables can help you understand how a piece of technology engages your attention. For instance, in the model shown in Table 2-2, the secondary attention channel is filled with audio, but there is still room for ambient sound.

TABLE 2-2. Attention model for a podcast

PRIMARY	SECONDARY	TERTIARY
Unused	Audio	*Unused*

In the attention model shown in Table 2-3, the primary focus is on the visual screen and touch navigation; the secondary proximal understanding of where you are in space is diminished, and ambient information around you is diminished or blocked. This is why someone can walk down the street while texting on a phone and almost walk into a wild bear (*https://www.youtube.com/watch?v=QCAntD1-DIk*), as a California man did in April 2012.

TABLE 2-3. Attention model for cell phone touchscreen use

PRIMARY	SECONDARY	TERTIARY
Visual screen and touch navigation	Diminished	Diminished or blocked

The attention model for driving is shown in Table 2-4. In this model, the attention is paid to oncoming traffic and traffic signals in the front window. This is why it is difficult to talk while driving, especially while merging onto a highway ramp. Your attention is almost entirely filled up with the primary and secondary channels.

TABLE 2-4. Attention model for driving

PRIMARY	SECONDARY	TERTIARY
Front window and general awareness of vehicle in space	Rearview mirrors, side windows, brake and acceleration pedal	Radio buttons, conversations with other people in the vehicle

Expanding on this, Table 2-5 shows the attention model for cell phone use while driving. In this mode, the primary, secondary, and tertiary information channels are consumed by the cell phone screen. The context shift takes precious moments away from driver responsiveness, making it difficult to adequately respond in time to prevent accidents or notice green lights or oncoming traffic. It is worth noting that the advent of automated cars will usher in an era of greater safety on the road. Individuals will be free to use phones while driving, as their primary focus will no longer be on the road but on the content in front of them. Automated cars will, in general, be much more capable drivers than humans, even when we are not distracted by something specific like a cell phone.

TABLE 2-5. Attention model for cell phone use while driving

PRIMARY	SECONDARY	TERTIARY
Visual screen and touch navigation; blocked: front window and general awareness of vehicle in space	Blocked: rearview mirrors, side windows; diminished attention to brake and acceleration pedal and street lights	Blocked: conversations and entire outside world diminished or blocked

Attention graphs

We can also introduce the concept of an attention graph. An attention graph can help you identify or plan out how a device captures attention over a period of time. Figure 2-4 illustrates the example of a teakettle. The attention is relatively high when the kettle is being set up, but diminishes when the user walks away from the kettle, and eventually the kettle is forgotten. When the kettle shouts, all attention is drawn to the kettle's state, and the user runs to pick it up.

FIGURE 2-4
Attention graph for a teakettle.

Our daily tech-saturated lives increasingly resemble the act of driving: there's a single, central task of crucial importance, but dozens of small, occasional supporting channels around it. Or perhaps, modern life is dysfunctional in part because it is more like trying to drive *many cars at once*, all of them pulled in their own separate directions and requiring lots of separate, individualized attention and product updates. Vehicle design has a lot to teach us about identifying and prioritizing primary and secondary tasks. Does an object require all of your attention to be focused right in front of you, or can you pay attention to it in the periphery? Acquiring **a good understanding of peripheral attention is essential to designing calm products.** We'll go over how to use the periphery in more detail in Chapter 3.

IV. TECHNOLOGY SHOULD AMPLIFY THE BEST OF TECHNOLOGY AND THE BEST OF HUMANITY

One of the hallmarks of poorly designed systems is that they force the human user to act like a machine in order to successfully complete a task. Machines shouldn't act like humans—at least, not in the current design environment that lacks the framework to effectively integrate "humanness" with devices—and humans shouldn't act like machines. Amplify the best of each, without expecting them to do each other's jobs. "Affective Computing" (*https://en.wikipedia.org/wiki/Affective_ computing*) involves studying and developing devices that can "recognize, interpret, process, and simulate human affects." The term was first introduced in 1995 by Rosalind Picard, professor of media arts and sciences at MIT. We'll say more about affective technology soon.

Think of the automatic faucet that turns on the water for you, but requires you to hold your hands in a very narrowly defined location during the entire process of washing—something few humans naturally do.

The best technology, on the other hand, **amplifies the best parts of both machines and people.** It never crosses their roles, or forgets who is who. All tech is designed by people at some point. The responsibility is on us to make it not just more efficient, but more accepting of the humanness of its users. **A person's primary task should not be computing; it should be being human.**

Being human means seeking food, fun, and social connection. It means improving the local environment, participating in the community, meeting or finding friends and family, participating in rituals or festivals. It means finding, creating, and performing meaningful work; learning constantly; and developing skills. Humans are problem solvers, but we also feel pain, love and friendship, jealousy, fear, happiness and joy. We feel a sense of accomplishment when we achieve our goals. We study religion and history, and ache for belonging.

We are also the ones who create the next steps in a field—something technology, by itself, cannot do. A machine can run a piece of code and even evolve that code if a human programs it to do so, but the human specialty of jumping a layer of abstraction and coming up with an insight that changes the fundamental way we do things is something that is unpredictable.

We have a history and a set of skills that we've developed in response to our culture and our environment. **Humans understand context.** Computers cannot understand context unless humans train them to. Originally the problem of teaching a machine to identify an object was thought to be a trivial task, but decades later it remains one of the most difficult problems in machine learning. Humans are still the best at object recognition, and machines can take those human insights and index them in order to make them available to other humans.

No matter how much human knowledge is put into a computer, it will never have the same needs as a living organism. It won't seek friendship or experience hunger, need to pee or clean itself. It doesn't care about its environment as long as it's able to function. Computers don't form families, or hang out in groups.

During the '90s, my father worked on voice concatenation systems (combining individual prerecorded words to create meaning) for a large telecom company in the Midwest. His task was to build a digital directory assistance system that allowed people to call a number and have an automated voice respond to it. First he worked with voice talent to record hundreds of thousands of words and phrases. Then he worked with linguists to stitch the words together so that text could be read back in a smooth and human-like way.

I used to sit at the dinner table and discuss artificial intelligence for hours with my dad. He didn't like the idea of artificial intelligence, and insisted on reading me bedtime stories from a pair of books called *The Evolution of Consciousness* by Robert E. Ornstein and *Naturally Intelligent Systems* by Maureen McHugh.

When my dad and I discussed voice recognition and automated systems, he would always point out how difficult these systems were to build: **"Computers don't have human forms. They don't grow up,"** he told me. "They don't understand what it's like to walk outside into the sun, or feel grass beneath their toes. They're a brain without a body. Because of that, they don't understand things the way that humans do. **The best thing computers can do is to connect humans to one another."**

What this ultimately got me to realize was that no computer can understand humans as well as we can understand one another. **Therefore, the best interfaces don't connect us to *technology*; they connect us to other people.** Google is indispensable not because it provides all the answers, but because it connects us to what others have discovered or written—and they have the answers. The Google interface itself is almost invisible. We don't look at it; we look at the search results. Google Search doesn't try to act human—it helps humans to find one another.

Google Search is an example of a system that amplifies humanness and makes the best use of a machine. You can think of it as a switchboard connecting humans to humans, through a series of bots that index the majority of human digital knowledge. Without bots indexing data, we could never find anything. Google doesn't determine the best result for us, but it does give us a series of results we can choose from, prioritized by their importance to other humans. From a given list of results, we can then understand which ones best pertain to our problem. The bots themselves only index human knowledge and help with the search results; they do not choose the result for us.

Mouse inventor Douglas Engelbart defined "augmenting human intellect" as the use of technology to increase the capability of people to be able to better approach complex problems and situations, to gain knowledge to suit specific needs, and to finally derive solutions to problems.[†] The lesson for designers and engineers is to **focus on optimizing your technology so that it amplifies the tasks that humans are better at that machines**; tasks like curation, working with context, understanding, being flexible, and improvisation. A computer

---

[†] Engelbart, Douglas. "Augmenting Human Intellect: A Conceptual Framework." *SRI Summary Report AFOSR-3223*, 1962. (*http://www.dougengelbart.org/pubs/augment-3906.html*)

can't truly understand or curate, and once it's been programmed, it's relatively inflexible. The better a system supports humans to do these things, the better the result!

These may seem like obvious differences, but they're worth acknowledging explicitly as we decide how to design the interactions between these two very different intelligences.

Designing affective technology

We know how to make products that are easy to use and understand. But what about emotions? What about designs that delight? What do we know about how to produce an emotional impact?
    DON NORMAN, AUTHOR, PROFESSOR, AND COFOUNDER OF NIELSEN NORMAN GROUP

Technology that is closest to interacting with humans as fully socio-emotional humans is *affective technology*. If we said before that **we are not bad at technology, technology is bad at us**, then affective technology is one of the most exciting opportunities for technology to be good at us, even including our socio-emotional "programming." It designs interfaces that account for human concerns such as usability, touch, access, persona, emotions, and personal history. This approach to devices can be exceptionally low-friction (if well designed), and **not only** *respects* **humans' limited amount of attention, but actually** *rewards it positively* **through constructive emotional reinforcement** from the technological device itself. The principles of affective technology represent a significant step in making an Internet of Things that is responsive and helpful to humans.

In Japan and elsewhere, many residents of nursing homes for the elderly seek companionship, but find none. Real companion animals are expensive, and difficult to feed and toilet train. Paro, shown in Figure 2-5, is a robotic companion in the shape of a baby harp seal. The robot has a touch sensor for petting and a light sensor for lightness and darkness in the environment. Posture and temperature sensors detect whether it is sitting on someone's lap or bed. Paro also has a direction-based auditory sensor to detect greetings and its own name.

FIGURE 2-5
Elderly residents in Japan with their Paro robotic seal companions.

Paro can be trained to increase or decrease a certain behavior by remembering whether it is stroked or punished for a specific action. The soft, robotic animal responds to interaction as if it were alive, by moving its head and legs and emitting the voice of a real baby harp seal. Paro is well loved in Japan. In addition to being the subject of a number of research studies proving its helpfulness, it is now a mainstay in many Japanese assisted living centers, and is especially helpful for residents living with dementia and depression. Paro provides animal companionship without the maintenance, and has a robotic body that universally responds to touch.

Affective technology can work with the needs of people and create experiences of delight. **Delight is something that can be achieved when the needs of humans and the interaction of technology are matched up.** In some cases, counter to what we said about non-affective technology in the previous section, it can work as a stand-in when a human resource is not available or nearby.

Guy Hoffman, now co-director of the media innovation lab at MIT, was inspired by the animation of the Pixar lamp to consider just how emotion could be built into robots and objects. He noticed that existing robotics possessed jerky and uncoordinated movements; it was difficult for people to identify with them. He strove to create robots with cleaner, more friendly and more "human" movements. Going to animation school and studying acting, he was able to build in more emotive reactions and "soft" movements into the robots. People interacting with them identified with them(as we do with anything properly anthropomorphised), finding them to be engaged, happy partners to work with.

FIGURE 2-6
Roboticist Guy Hoffman with one of his "Robots with Soul." Illustration by the author.

V. TECHNOLOGY CAN COMMUNICATE, BUT DOESN'T NEED TO SPEAK

One of the most common, and most vexing, examples of technology trying to emulate humans is the disembodied voice. **As voice-based interfaces become more common, it's worth addressing the problems with voice interaction specifically,** which is why it gets its own Calm Design principle.

A couple of years ago, I had a conversation with one of the cofounders of Siri. We talked about how Siri was "trained" on a Californian English vocal pattern and accent, because that's where Siri was designed. Within minutes, Siri's cofounder started showing me videos in which Siri completely fails to understand users, despite them lacking any trace of an accent that differs from Siri's own. This kind of experience can be uniquely frustrating for users, because it forces them to modify their own behavior for the benefit of a machine, but the machine is only demanding such contortions because it's trying to "communicate like a human." **Making a computer speak like a human without instilling it with a sense of human context or relationships ultimately leads to a sense of dissonance in the person using it**—exactly what affective design is seeking to remedy.

Siri is still considered a failure by some groups because it was advertised as having far more accurate capabilities than it turned out to have. We're accustomed to hearing computer voices in movies, but movies have post-production. They are polished and cut to look perfect. Real life doesn't work that way. Many of us have been led to believe we can have computers as accurate as the ship's computer in *Star Trek*, but that voice is a carefully scripted plot device intended to help bring the computer to life in a way that looks (and performs) better than text on a screen. The computer voice lets the device be a part of the action instead of a simple terminal. When we watch these films, we get used to the idea of talking to a computer, even though the idea of human–computer communication relies much more on context than we realize.

One of the biggest draws for robotic voice systems is the idea that they could anticipate our emotional and physical needs without judgment. They could be our faithful servants and provide unwavering emotional support. And while there are some examples of Japanese virtual boyfriend and girlfriend systems, as well as the virtual chatbot psychologists of early days, the best way to train an AI system is by connecting it to human context. The Google Search engine does this well. Google uses bots to index content created by people and provides suggested search results. In the end, it is the human that decides what site is more relevant to them. Google just does a bit of the heavy lifting.

Voice interfaces rarely work, for the same reason that visual interfaces at the center of our field of vision rarely work (Principle II): they both require the majority of our limited attention. As we discussed in

Principle II, the path to calmer interaction is primarily about presenting information *in parallel*, and matching the information density of the interaction with the channel through which it communicates.

A user interface requiring all of our visual focus distracts us from doing anything else. An interface that requires our complete auditory focus (or perfect enunciation) is equally distracting. In the absence of audible interfaces, consider making use of tones or lights or sensory stimulation to get the point across.

Voice recognition works best in a quiet environment, but most environments are not quiet. I once watched a woman get frustrated while attempting to use a voice-recognition system at a kiosk in an airport. Halfway through the automated menu, the noise of her kids, combined with the background noise of the airport paging system, threw her back to the beginning of the menu, interrupting her progress and forcing her to do it all over again. An auditory-based machine on a busy street faces similar problems.

Or take the example of a parking ticket machine that uses a prerecorded human voice to communicate. First, it speaks in a slow, disjointed voice that's more disorienting than helpful. Second, it takes your card but offers no feedback of whether the transaction went through. Third, if nothing happens, there is no call button to ask for help from a person, and no person nearby. People get stuck in parking lots this way—a deeply disconcerting experience that puts the user, not the machine, on pause (the next principle addresses this issue directly).

Human voice, then, should be used only when absolutely necessary. Introducing a voice creates a variety of new issues: the need for stringing together words in voice "concatenation," the near certainty of misinterpretation, or the accent issue that Siri so clearly demonstrates. Human voices must also be translated into multiple languages for accessibility purposes, while **a simple positive or negative tone, symbol, or light can be designed in a way that's universally understood.**

Instead, create ambient awareness through different senses. **Use a status tone instead of a spoken voice. Use a buzz instead of a voice-based alert. Use a status light instead of a display.** If done well, a simple light or tone can clearly convey information without forcing users to pay all of their attention.

One example might be the light status indicator you find on a convection stove after the stove is turned off, but the surface is still hot. This indicator is not necessary on gas stoves, as the burners quickly cool down when the gas is turned off. Another example is the recording indicator light on a standard video camera.

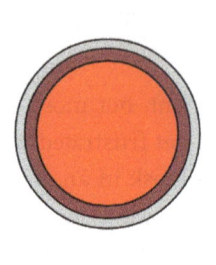

Hot Surface   Rec

A. Stove indicator light   **B.** Video camera light

FIGURE 2-7
Examples of various light status indicators.

Many of us remember the brief period in the 1980s when several car makers, led by BMW, started putting voice alerts in their cars to convey extremely simple messages. Suddenly, showrooms around the world were full of luxury cars saying, "Your door is ajar! Your door is ajar!" every time you left the door open. Consumer response was swift, strong, and decidedly negative—nobody wants to be lectured by their car, and a speaking voice is overkill for such a basic piece of information. BMW switched to a gentle, wordless tone the following year, other makers followed suit, and now the talking car door is just a footnote, and the subject of a handful of '80s-era comedy sketches.

Getting the alert tone right takes careful consideration. There's no question that our day-to-day technological lives are currently filled with too much beeping and buzzing, but this is largely a result of how those alerts are designed. It's still rare to find an audible alert that uses a calming tone. Most are sharp and distracting—a result, most often, of the hubris of designers and engineers who believe that *their* technology's alert is the most important thing in the user's environment, so it must be unmistakable. But getting a loud buzz for every email, status update, and news item quickly makes every buzz meaningless. Strive to match the urgency of the tone with the urgency of the alert, and recognize that many pieces of information aren't time-sensitive enough to need one.

The Roomba robotic vacuum cleaner, for example, emits a happy tone when cleaning is complete, and a sad tone when it gets stuck. **The tone is unambiguous but unintrusive, and needs no translation.** Additionally, a light display on the Roomba shows green when clean and orange when dirty or stuck.

Where does voice interaction make sense, then? Under certain controlled circumstances, where it's reliably quiet, where the task is simple, or where a tone doesn't convey enough information. Also, where there are clear benefits to not having to look at or touch your device. Turn-by-turn interactive directions while driving are the most common and most successful example of this kind of interaction.

A car is a closed, quiet, and controlled environment. Driving directions follow a very consistent format, but differ in content every time. More important, driving is an activity that demands complete visual attention, making a strong safety case for voice interaction. Audible driving directions aren't chatty or quirky; they provide a secondary focus that can help someone reliably get to a destination without being distracted from the road. A vehicle is a realm in which the user's humanness isn't really at stake in the same way, so ignoring social and emotional cues is perfectly acceptable. It seems to be a principle of parsimony, or "minimal technology."

Smartphones that use voice interaction successfully also take advantage of pre-inputted information—for example, learning what address constitutes "home," then letting the user simply say "give me directions home" and resolving it to the address.

We've already talked extensively about using the periphery to convey information in parallel. But if you have three types of peripheral notification—visual, haptic ("related to touch or proprioception") and audible—**when do you know when to use which?**

The answer is context.

Where is the tech going to be used? Is it a loud environment? A quiet one? A messy one? A dark or light one? If it's in bright sun, the user might not be able to see an indicator light. If it's a personal notification, a haptic notification might be the most appropriate. Haptic notifications can consist of anything that involves a sense of touch, including texture, braille, vibration, electricity, or temperature. A haptic alert can be very useful for personal notifications, as touch has the greatest proximity of any alert. A haptic alert can be configured to allow just one person to feel it, especially if it's a personal device worn on the user's body. A calm alert is almost always better than a sharp one: a haptic buzz doesn't have to be intense, a light doesn't have to be blinding, and a tone doesn't have to be obnoxiously loud.

Sometimes having two notifications is useful, as it increases the likelihood of the user noticing it without demanding their full attention.

As a primary notification method, simulated human voice has many downsides. Sometimes, it is justified and necessary, but often it can be replaced by something simpler, calmer, and more appropriate. Think very hard about why you might need to put a human voice into a product, and first consider if any of the other alerts described in Chapter 3 might be more appropriate. If there's a better way to do it, don't hesitate to change how the product communicates with the user!

VI. TECHNOLOGY SHOULD WORK EVEN WHEN IT FAILS

An airplane whose engines have failed defaults to a glider. On the less catastrophic side of things, escalators are more resilient than elevators because they revert to stairs when they stop working.

This mindset should govern the design of technology as much as possible. Designers and developers tend to focus their efforts on the use cases that they foresee as most common, putting tremendous thought into how they might make these cases work faster and more smoothly. This is necessary and admirable, but it does little to address the cases when failure is most likely to occur.

The edge cases are where things go wrong. When users try to do something unusual with the technology, or get to an outcome without going through all the correct steps, that's when failure tends to strike, and calmness disappears.

There's a strong temptation for designers and developers to shrug these cases off, either because they're too rare to address, or the result of a user that's "too dumb," but the fact is that **everyone is an edge case at one time or another.** Sometimes it's because they're just learning the technology, and don't realize exactly what's expected of them. Sometimes they have an unusual need and they're trying to stretch the tech's capabilities. Sometimes—as in the example discussed in "The False Alarm That Wouldn't Stop"—it's not their fault at all, and they're just trying to deal with a rare but unpleasant exception.

The problem with edge cases is that their impact far outweighs their frequency. Hue is a lighting system developed by Philips that gives users unprecedented control over the lighting in their homes, through a well-designed app that governs a system of adjustable-color LEDs. When it works—which is the vast majority of the time—it's quite magical, and the setup and installation are surprisingly straightforward. But in 2014, if you asked Hue owners about their systems, most of them would probably tell you about the time that it crashed, leaving them with a house full of lights at full brightness, and no obvious way to turn them off.

A bug in the most recent automatic firmware update was the culprit, and once alerted, Philips did a decent job of rushing the patch in...but try telling that to a family trying to go to sleep in a fully lit bedroom.

In fact, there was a temporary fix: you could simply turn the lights off at the wall switch. But many users, accustomed to controlling their lights via the app, didn't realize this. Philips eventually announced the fact via the Hue Twitter account, and apologized profusely, but the damage had been done. Thousands of users were left with the uneasy feeling that *the lights in their house could crash,* and Philips has struggled to rebuild the faith ever since.

What the designers should have done was anticipated this edge case, and built **language** into their marketing materials. When a user is untrained for what to do during a technology failure, confidence in a product can shatter.

We, as humans, hate bumping up against these kinds of gaps in the user experience because they lay bare the difference between people and machines. People have a built-in capacity for flexibility and empathy, and machines don't, so "crashing" is about the least human thing a piece of technology can do.

When you design, put yourself in the shoes of your users—**not just the competent, experienced users doing the thing you want them to do**, but the users just figuring it out, pushing the edges, or dealing with a bug. A simple "off" switch can work wonders. So can a fallback mode that offers less functionality but easier access to the basics.

In general, though, **the key to dealing with edge cases is providing redundancy**. Make sure your system can still work when a portion of it fails, and give users a choice of options for getting crucial tasks done. Designing and building multiple parallel action paths may not feel like the most efficient solution, but then, neither is training jet pilots to fly a glider.

The False Alarm That Wouldn't Stop

A few months ago, I saw an update from Facebook friend and author William Hertling on a false alarm from his Nest smoke detector (Figure 2-8). The device gave him a lot of trouble before he was able to turn it off.

FIGURE 2-8

The Internet-connected Nest smoke detector and the mobile Nest control application.

Hertling reported "three piercing loud beeps, and then a voice saying 'Smoke detected in the entranceway. Smoke detected in the entranceway.' There were five Nest smoke detectors in the house, all of them doing the same thing, all slightly out of sync with each other, so you hear a weird echoing of the beeps and the announcement about 2-4 seconds apart."

Was there any way to stop the alarm, or disassemble it?

"At first I could silence it," Hertling said, "but then it started again, and said **'This alarm can not be silenced.'** If it had been a cheaper smoke detector, I might have smashed it on the sidewalk outside. But, of course, it's stupendously expensive, so I wasn't about to do that. To try to find the right size screwdriver and disassemble this thing calmly, without any coffee, and with alarms blaring all over the place, kids evacuating the house and trying to find things to put cats in, it was not an easy task." That's not even the only trouble Nest systems have run into. *Wired* reported in April 2014: "After a nearly blemish-free record that culminated in a $3 billion acquisition by Google, Nest today issued a surprising halt to sales of Protect, its gesture-controlled smoke alarm. One of the device's key features was that you could wave at it to turn it off. Turns out, other movements might also mute the alarm inadvertently.* Thus, as CEO Tony Fadell put it, 'This could delay the alarm going off if there was a real fire.' Oops."

Why not have a simple button that stops the alarm? A button is simple to press, and easy for a computer to understand. There's no ambiguity in intent. The product was designed well in general, but missed a core interactive feature: "How do you turn the alarm off?" Sometimes, companies with exceptional design practices can miss the most basic interactions. Testing your device in many different environments is a way to help prevent this.

VII. THE RIGHT AMOUNT OF TECHNOLOGY IS THE MINIMUM NEEDED TO SOLVE THE PROBLEM

Perfection is achieved, not when there is nothing more to add, but when there is nothing left to take away.
   ANTOINE DE SAINT-EXUPERY

All products might begin as a simple idea, but bringing that idea to life involves a series of complex processes and design decisions. Designing a simple thing often requires a complicated process.

A product that utilizes the right amount of technology becomes invisible more quickly, which is **a hallmark of effective Calm Design**. When a product works with us in our existing environment, and fits into our existing workflow, we begin to ignore it, or take it for granted. This may sound defeatist, but the alternative is far worse: using poorly designed tech is like solving a story problem every time we use it. It requires us, the users, to adapt to clunky technology and find the features we actually need to use.

But while good technology is often simple, a good design process almost never is. **Good designers aren't afraid of working through all the tiny details and all the edge cases they can conceive, removing unnecessary features until there is nothing left to take away.** They design with the fewest number of components, because more features make for more failures, and complex systems leave more room for security faults.

For hardware products, **good design means fewer things that can break**, easier assembly, and fewer failed units. It means less physical tech support, shorter onboarding, and a more beloved product. Each new feature must be developed, tested, explained to the market, and then supported. It must also be updated when underlying systems change. Add a feature only when absolutely necessary.

Apple's Complex Path to Simplicity

In an interview in the 2009 documentary *Objectified* by Gary Hustwit, Apple's Jony Ive spends several minutes explaining the amount of work his team puts into reducing the part count on each generation of Mac. Through a complex series of machining steps, they had been able to replace dozens of separate parts with physical features that are built into a laptop's aluminum chassis, which contributes greatly to its sense of solidity and simplicity. The result feels simple, but the process that produced it is incredibly complex.

Similarly, eliminating the CD-ROM drive was something that initially earned Apple tremendous criticism when they released the first MacBook Air. This elimination allowed them to create a streamlined, lightweight computer, which has since achieved success in the market—but it was only possible because of the massive, years-long efforts that Apple and other companies had put into streaming media, faster web connections, and cloud storage. because of the massive, years-long efforts that Apple and other companies had put into streaming media, faster web connections, and cloud storage.

Dieter Rams famously said that **"good design is as little design as possible"** many decades ago, and designers have been quoting him ever since. So if we all know it and agree with it, why are we often so reluctant to actually deliver on simplicity?

In part, it's because of speed. It's often faster to build a feature-laden product than a streamlined one, because adding something new without evaluating what's already there is a fairly straightforward process. Complexity is also a management issue. We often empower managers and directors to add features, but very few people have the authority to take them away.

In the digital world, complexity also arises out of conflict between legacy systems and newer technologies. We may try to use a new programming language that everyone's talking about, but we don't take into account that it, too, will be legacy one day, and that the designers who work on the next iteration will be reluctant to deal with the "old" code, just as we are today.

Every product starts out complicated. Life is complex, reality is complex, and you're no longer designing for a desktop sitting in a simplified, isolated bubble. When your product is competing with many others in an unpredictable environment, you must design for a complex system. This means abstracting the insights gained from your research and the concepts developed in your design process so that the user is left with the simplest possible product that can be used. This doesn't mean doing the user's tasks for them. It means **empowering the user to get to their goal with the least amount of attention.**

What problem does your system solve? For each new feature, **ask yourself,** *is this something necessary to the product?* **Not fun, but** *necessary*. If it doesn't solve a core problem, *don't build it*. Even if managers and stakeholders get in the way, you can always have them answer these core questions.

The technology in our homes offers a good example. Home technology systems include many components—lights and switches, outlets, breakers, major appliances, heating and cooling systems, etc.—and they all work pretty well. Everyone basically knows how to use all of the components (even the more exotic ones, like dimmers and fan controls), and can adjust them to their needs. This is largely because interfaces are fairly obvious, and provide direct feedback on the outcome, whether it's a light coming on or a kettle getting hot. It's also because the systems are extremely standardized: practically any homeowner can quickly figure out any house.

There's much more behind the scenes. Home wiring diagrams can become very complicated, very quickly, which is one of the reasons electricians have to go through long periods of training, apprenticeship, and accreditation before they're allowed to work on your home. That complexity, though, is designed to ensure safety and reliability, and to minimize additional interaction demands on the user.

But suppose you want to control your lights using a remote control, or your phone. Perhaps you find an exciting new system on Kickstarter that you want to fund, or maybe you buy some Hue lights and install them. Then suppose you want to get into your home by pressing a few buttons rather than using a key, and you install SmartThings so you can trigger your lights to turn on when you enter a room.

Suddenly, you have a lot of new complexity, and it's not just behind the scenes. Your various software systems don't always work well together, because they don't adhere to a consistent set of standards. You forget to update the system. You leave town for a couple of weeks and the entry system's batteries run flat so you can't get into your own house. Or you set up the systems a year ago in a fervor of excitement and have forgotten which parts go where, so you end up living in a home that is slowly breaking down on you. Or you break up with your partner and they move out of your house, but still have access to all of the shared home tech accounts; suddenly your ex knows when you enter and leave your home, and gets push notifications every time you weigh yourself on your connected scale.

Both of the systems described here are complex, but the second one isn't standardized, nor is it optimized for calm interactivity. It does offer more functionality, but only by shifting most of the interaction demand to the user.

There is a tendency in the tech world for technical capability to race ahead of reliability. We do not install electrical systems with the expectation that the homeowner can fix every system in the house, or rewire it if something breaks down, and that influences how we install them in the first place. It's not just a matter of using the least amount of tech possible, but of building that tech in such a way that the complexity is, to some degree, self-policing—that's why home electrical systems have ground wires, waterproof outdoor outlets, and dimmers placed next to the relevant switches.

You shouldn't have to be a system administrator to live in your own home. And you shouldn't have to *have* a system administrator either. I am not condemning the home automation hobbyist here, but in order for home automation to become widespread, it needs to be as reliable as electricity. A current automated home remote control system can take up to four steps to turn on the lights: for most of us, a light switch is better. The Hue customizable lighting system now offers HueTap, a wireless light switch that mounts to your wall or is set on your desk. Crucially, it's powered by the kinetic energy of pressing the buttons, so it doesn't require batteries.

Such small positive steps illuminate a guiding principle of Calm Technology: **don't introduce new dependencies unless there's no other way.** Instead of a remote control or dedicated app, why not *text* your house? Every phone already has a text message system, but not all phones can run every kind of app. If a technology relies on the newest mobile technology, it may break with the next software upgrade. But if it works via text message or a physical button, it has a longer interaction lifetime, and a shorter learning curve.

In general, when you design technology, consider the lifetime of the interaction models you use with it, and introduce a new mode of interaction only as a last resort. 95% of the time, there's already an existing level of interaction that the user is familiar with and that satisfies your interaction needs. Put your design efforts into making that work right, not always into creating a new gadget that can crash.

VIII. TECHNOLOGY SHOULD RESPECT SOCIAL NORMS

A society's cultural norms define the social forces that push humans to interact in a way that is congruent with accepted social rules. Else, the individual may encounter what sociologist Erving Goffman describes as "losing face."[‡] Our interactions with technology are not exempt: every device and tool comes with societal expectations that tell us how

---

[‡] Goffman, Erving. *Interaction Ritual: Essays on Face to Face Behavior.* 1st Pantheon Books ed. New York: Pantheon Books, 1982.

and when they're acceptable to use. **When we talk about a socially "normal" technology, what we really mean is one that conforms with existing norms, or (more often) one that our norms have adjusted to accept.**

Marc Weiser wrote that "the most profound technologies are those that disappear. They weave themselves into the fabric of everyday life until they are indistinguishable from it."[§] An accepted technology becomes **unremarkable**, to the point where it is effectively invisible. In much of the urbanized world, a smartphone is one such technology. We don't take a second glance at someone using a smartphone today, even though it would have been quite astonishing to watch someone tapping away at a mobile screen 10 years ago.

This process of cultural "metabolization" takes place at different rates for different technologies, and for some technologies it never happens at all. The smartphone took just a year or two to seem normal, while Google Glass is still creepy three years after release, and the Segway remains a joke after a decade.

Journalism can act as a catalyst for metabolization, but the creators of the technology are also responsible for the task of designing its message in a way that minimizes fear and dismissiveness. They also need to serve up new features in a digestible size, so that users aren't bombarded with too many shifts at once.

One of the easiest ways for a technology to be metabolized is if it's perceived as **restoring people to the norm**. Eyeglasses are not fear inducing, and neither are wheelchairs or crutches, because they give people capabilities that put them back in line with what's considered "normal." If a technology is seen as enhancing, on the other hand—if it promises to elevate someone's capabilities beyond "normal"—the reaction to it is more likely to be fear. So part of the task of creating messaging for new technologies lies in **expanding people's definition of "normal." This is almost always a gradual process.**

Can you imagine the early reaction to the telephone? It was magical and exciting, of course, but also a dramatically unfamiliar experience. Some people couldn't imagine the idea of a person going into a room

---

§ Weiser, Mark. "The Computer for the Twenty-First Century." *Scientific American* 265, no. 9 (1991): 66-75.

alone and talking to another person far away. In fact, many at the time were **worried that telephones would lead to social isolation and depression**. But after they started showing up in people's businesses and homes, calling people far away became the norm, and the telephone was seen as a **connector**, not an isolator.

The telephone was metabolized in a very gradual way, over the course of decades, and it helped that it began with public telephones in places like post offices and banks, to make the technology feel "under control" and less intimidating. It also helped that it was building on the precedent set by the telegraph. By the time the first telephone exchanges were opening in the 1880s, the telegraph had been in operation for more than 40 years, and "reported via telegraph" was a common notation in the newspapers Americans and Europeans read every day. This helped the telephone feel like a next step, not a complete disruption.

A similar revolution happened with the advent of the mobile phone camera. Neither the cell phone nor the digital camera were new technologies, but when the two were combined, a certain paranoia set in. Now people could take pictures discreetly anywhere. Camera phones were banned from locker rooms, even offices. **Papers were written about the end of privacy.** People were upset, but 5–10 years later, camera phones have become the norm.

What happened? Everyone bought one. **The social action of taking a photo became commonplace**, whether at a family gathering, a concert, or a restaurant. The ability for anyone to take a picture at any time made the entire concept mundane, and that made it feel safe.

In 2005, Apple began working on a mobile phone that offered a new method of interaction: a large, multi-touch touchscreen. It wasn't the first phone with Internet capabilities, but it did allow a much clearer view of the Web than any previous mobile device. Suddenly the Web became enjoyable on the phone, and there were apps, too—but not at first. Let's take a closer look at how the product evolved.

On June 29, 2007, Steve Jobs introduced what at the time seemed like a ridiculous product to the world. It was an iPhone (see Figure 2-9). A solid piece of metal and glass that was like a smooth stone about the size of your hand. Inside this strange device were some built-in apps like a web browser and a very low-resolution camera.

FIGURE 2-9

The Apple home page in January 2007, at the time of the first iPhone launch—the first version of the iPhone shipped with a handful of built-in iPhone apps, Apple maps, a web browser with a "mobile" view of the *New York Times*, a music player, and a phone interface.

Consumers were a little shocked. Where was the keyboard? Why was the screen the full size of the device? Why would Apple make a phone? It seemed like a huge risk. And the price was outrageous! One thing was for sure—only a few people were going to buy this thing (or rather, some tech writers quipped, beta test it). It didn't seem like a good idea at all. But it was.

At first, the iPhone was an expensive luxury item, **allowing its supply chain to start small and build up as demand increased.** In 2008, Apple introduced an improved iPhone at a lower price point, and the phone came with another new capability: the ability to download apps developed by third parties. At that point, customers were familiar with what an iPhone could do, and any team of developers could pay $99 to get early access to Apple's developer tools and build apps in anticipation of the next phone's release. Before long, developers started showing up from all over. Fourteen-year-olds made silly apps. **A whoopee cushion app caused headlines and mirth.** This playfulness helped demonstrate the features that made the iPhone unique, **but it also made it feel less frightening.** The developers, along with news sites and early adopters, told the story—not Apple.

The iPhone's core hardware continued to improve. Every season, a new set of improvements and capabilities were introduced, and everyone got to learn about the new features at the same time, build new categories of software using them, and communicate the new features to one another. The App Store grew and grew with each new release, ushering in a whole new set of developers and an entirely new way to make money. Young developers, some just barely teenagers, could post tutorials on YouTube and teach people to code. Documentation was written by users and added to over time. As of mid-2015, over 1.5 million apps were listed on the App Store, and 100+ billion apps have been downloaded.

Apple's iPhone became a market leader because it improved on what was already out there. The first iPhone improved the user interface standards set by a market dominated by Nokia, Blackberry, Palm, and Windows Mobile phones. All of these devices had a physical keyboard. While useful for emails and text messages, the keyboards took up roughly half of the device. By allowing the keyboard to dissolve and reappear on the screen, the iPhone could make use of a much larger screen size. This opened up an industry-changing shift—the ability to make full-screen, full-touch applications.

It still took many years for the iPhone to come to maturity, but imagine if Apple had released an iPhone with apps, location awareness, multi-tasking, and a large screen all at once? The price point would have been outrageous, **the device completely alien**, and the smartphone almost certainly a disastrous failure. Give people one feature or concept at a time, per season, so users can readjust to the idea and it can become the norm. Otherwise you might be stuck with an amalgamation of random features, many of which will not be functional for your users. And if you're making a physical product, it gives your supply chain a chance to breathe, improve, and evolve.

Google Glass, shown in Figure 2-10, failed for exactly this reason. When Glass launched in 2013, developers had to pay $1,600 USD and be invited by Google in order to buy a device and start building applications for it. **Without many people capable of doing this, it became mysterious**, and certainly not an object of play. It also included a broad array of features released all at once, making for a big marketing splash but very little focus, and a lot of confusion and concern.

Without a clear feature to focus on, public opinion seized on its own concern: the idea that anyone wearing Glass was recording everyone all the time. Glass didn't have a recording indicator light, as essentially every other video recording device up to that point had. This omission created ambiguity, leading many people to assume that any

Glass-wearer was persistently recording—when in fact, after 15–20 minutes of video, it got too hot and the battery ran out. For about six weeks in 2014, I wore Glass constantly, all around the world, in groups of people from a wide range of social classes, age groups, and nationalities. By far the most common first question I received was, "are you recording me right now?"

FIGURE 2-10
Developer Brennan Novak tries out my pair of Google Glass at a bar in Brighton, England, at the height of "Google Glass mania" in September 2013.

If you took all of the articles about feature phones with cameras from the 2000s and replaced the word "camera" with "Glass," you'd have the same articles on Google Glass we saw in 2014. As with cameraphones, there will eventually be a new set of social rules to govern head-wearable devices, but we're not there yet. Wearing Glass gives you a lot of power, but you also have to explain the limits of that power to others, and many of us are fundamentally uncomfortable with the idea of wearing a camera on our faces. Sometimes it's better just to leave it off.

Additionally, Google created **a closed system** that couldn't be hacked or played with, meaning that all excitement about and discovery of the product was blocked. The so-called "Explorers" program Google launched with Glass didn't actually allow people to explore the product because its use cases were actually fairly limited.

To make a successful product launch, it's crucial to study your audience, their social cues, and the local culture around technology, to ensure that you understand why people might or might not want your product. Release features slowly until they are adopted by the general public, and provide a way for people to play with your product and become comfortable with it.

Calm Technology lives in the real world, among people. Respect their expectations, and they'll respect your technology.

Conclusions

Although the principles discussed in this chapter cover a wide range of behaviors and expectations, they generally revolve around three key considerations: attention, reliability, and context. Designing Calm Technology requires that we respect human attention for the valuable commodity it is, that we make our technology so reliable that we don't have to expend cognitive energy on its base functioning, and that we always take into account the context in which it's used.

These ideas are familiar in human-centered design, social design, and anthropology. All of the other principles flow from them.

It's never too late.

It is important to realize that making technology "calm" is an ongoing process—it's a set of values that inform decision making, rather than an algorithm that governs a phase of your project. Learn the principles now and look for opportunities to apply them in your products, new and existing.

You can always "calm down" existing technology by compressing notifications into different forms or using different notification styles. You can always reduce the feature set on your next release; you can always replace a visual display with a tone, a visual indicator, or a moment of haptic feedback. You can always mine the history of your technology's category for ideas of what's accessible and acceptable.

The principles of Calm Technology discussed in this chapter can be applied through the use of status indicators and alerts. In the next chapter, we'll discuss different types of status indicators and alert styles that you can use in your products to make technology take up less attention.

These are the key takeaways from this chapter:

- Keep in mind that people have a limited amount of attention. Attempt to create technology that requires the least amount of their attention while providing the most useful functions.
- Consider how your interface can provide information without taking the user out of their primary task.

- Explore ways in which your technology can make use of peripheral attention. Technology should make use of the periphery.

- Consider how your product amplifies a person's natural strengths and uses the capabilities of technology to reduce the human load.

- Does your product need to rely on voice, or can it use a different communication method? Consider how your technology communicates status.

- Think about what happens if your technology fails. Does it default to a usable state or does it break down completely?

- What is the minimum amount of technology needed to solve the problem? Slim the feature set down so that the product does what it needs to do and no more.

- What social norms exist that your technology might violate or cause stress on? Ideally, people should feel good when they interact with the product.

[3]

Calm Communication Patterns

THIS CHAPTER IS ABOUT communication patterns that can help to "calm down" an otherwise overly demanding interaction or interface. While not prescriptive, it describes a variety of communication modes that often feature in well-designed Calm Technology, and uses examples of existing technology as well as theoretical or experimental products to illustrate how they work. We will discuss indicator types, ambient awareness, contextual notifications, and persuasive technology. There are enough examples here that you may find something that parallels a project you're currently working on. More broadly, reading through the various examples should help establish patterns that do a better job of showing how calm interaction works than any kind of theoretical explanation could.

Status indicators and contextual notifications are worth special attention, not because they are the sum total of technological interaction, but because **technology is most likely to be *uncalm* in the way it announces itself.** They are also the aspects of design most often left to chance, or default. Designers often implement visual alerts or default tones without really thinking about how they could affect people *in context*. Being able to choose from a greater range of status indicators can help lead to products that are **pleasant to use** rather than stereotypically difficult.

The final section is reserved for persuasive technology, a crucial theoretical construct that is ignored by far too many designers of software and devices. It's important to remember that as technology becomes increasingly embedded in daily life, it maintains conversations with its users. When we talk about smartphones and wearables, we usually mean devices that are always on, always listening, and frequently reacting to us without our initiating contact. This brings great potential for making life easier, and for making life more complicated. Understanding how the feedback cycle works is crucial to making the former outcome more likely.

Status Indicators

The status indicators we'll discuss include standard indicators—visual, auditory, and touch-based haptic indicators—and what I term "status shouts."

In this book, I focus on indicators that make use of vision, sound, and touch, because they are the most common and easy to use when creating technological devices. Of course, both taste and smell are sensory alerts that can be used to create Calm Technology, too. Those who wish to stop biting their nails can coat them with a harmless bitter lacquer that acts as a deterrent. This is an exceptional use of a sensory alert: the taste only happens when the behavior in question is being produced, and otherwise, the technology is perfectly unnoticeable. Smells from the kitchen can send people running in to eat. A fresh scent in an office building or lobby can help people feel at ease. Perfume is an early Calm Technology that uses a nuanced smell to encourage romance, and scented markers for children have won over back-to-school shoppers. The Chili's franchise hit the jackpot with its sizzling chicken fajita dish because the smell coupled with the crackling sound of food cooking on a cast iron pan spurred people to order the dish.

There are literally dozens of ways that technologies can let us know that something has happened or that something is wrong—pop-up boxes, text alerts, dialogs, flashing lights, banners, bell and whistles.

I'd like to focus on the ones that I've found most associated with technologies that are considered "calm" and that work with the user's life in the best way. It's not that information should never be presented in pop-up boxes or text alerts, but there may be other methods to consider before implementing full displays, and ways to make those aspects a secondary system. With a status light, for instance, users can know to check a system when the light changes color instead of needing to check it all of the time to determine its status.

These are a few approaches you should try out first before you consider other, less calm approaches.

VISUAL STATUS INDICATORS

A status light is perhaps the calmest way of conveying a piece of information. It's also the lowest resolution of all status indicators—at its simplest, a single LED that transmits one bit of information: on or off.

Status lights are ideal for communicating low-importance, persistent information. As discussed in the previous chapter, the group messaging system Slack lets you know there are messages to read by adding a blue dot to the app's icon. This creates an intentionally low-res way of communicating, especially compared with pop-up boxes or the "You've got mail!" announcements of years past.

Our daily lives are actually filled with status lights. They carry more information with less distraction than any other status indicator.

Status lights can also convey deeper information through multiple colors and varying levels of brightness. Factor in the ability to turn a status light into a shape or icon, or associate text with it, and you have a powerful visual indicator with relatively little attention load. But lights are not the only visual indicators—seeing when a container is full of liquid (or empty), or when a tomato turns red, can be useful, low-tech visual indicators.

Consider the following:

Heat light on a stove
> One of the most basic examples of a status light is the heat light on a stove that tells you when a burner is on. A more advanced heat light may signal that the burner is still hot after it's been turned off, adding useful information without additional complexity.

Bedtime lamp
> When I was young, my parents got tired of arguing with me about my bedtime. To solve this problem, my dad plugged a programmable device called an X10 controller into the wall outlet. He plugged a lamp into it and set it to turn on every evening at 8:30pm. When I hung out with my parents in the living room, I simply scampered off to bed when the light turned on, saving considerable fuss. It soon became a part of my life, just as if my parents had told me it was time for bed—the difference being that I couldn't argue with the light as I could with my parents.

Server status light
> A status light is an easy way for teams to be aware of how a server is operating without looking at monitoring software. In many cases, this is done with rope lights, strung along a wall or ceiling that's visible to the engineering team: if the build is good and the server

is up, the rope is green; if it has an issue that needs attending to, it's yellow; if the server needs immediate attention or has gone down, the rope shows red.

Light-based faucet

An MIT paper from 2005 proposed a light-based faucet (Figure 3-1) that could change color based on water temperature, turning red when the water was hot and turning blue when the water was cold. This replaces the sense of touch with a visual display, indicating water temperature without having to check it with a hand, thereby avoiding burns. Temperature-sensing glow faucets and shower heads are now available in the online marketplace Amazon.com.

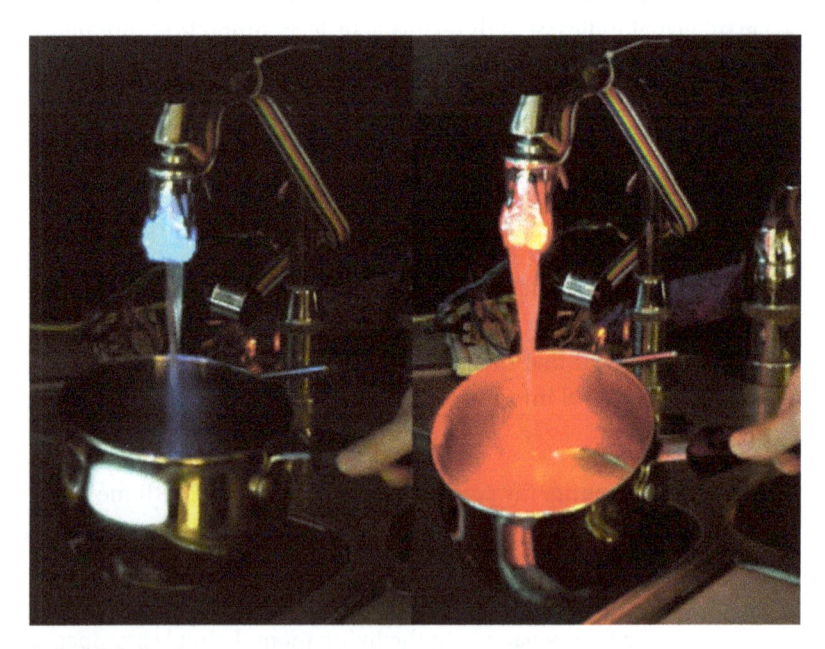

FIGURE 3-1

HeatSink. This LED-powered water faucet attachment indicates visually whether the temperature is hot or cool.*

---

* Bonanni, Leonardo, Chia-Hsun Lee, and Ted Selker. "Attention-Based Design of Augmented Reality Interfaces." *Proc. CHI 2005.* (*https://web.archive.org/web/20051108192401/http://web.media.mit.edu/~jackylee/publication/lbr-484-bonanni.pdf*)

Why Car Radios Still Have Knobs

I was told anecdotally at a technology conference about an in-vehicle touchscreen that was tested in a lab setting, but never with a driver on the road. This system was completely distracting and almost impossible to use. In a vehicle, having simple tactile controls (physical buttons, sliders, rotating knobs) allows your brain to remember where they are without forcing you to look at them. You can turn the radio on and off without taking your eyes off of the road. You can feel for where a radio or CD player button is. But bright touchscreens in vehicle dashboards can distract drivers from the road while driving at night. Being able to quickly turn down the brightness of the screen with a physical dial is critical, not just to comfort but to safety as well.

Light-up toothbrush

> You may be familiar with some electronic toothbrushes that stay on for the recommended two minutes and then buzz to let you know you're finished, but what about a toothbrush that lets you know when you've forgotten to brush your teeth entirely? Imagine a toothbrush with a handle or small indicator that lights up when you haven't brushed your teeth that morning or evening. The light stays on until you've used it for the recommended period of time, then resets to light up at the next scheduled time.
>
> The Virtual Aquarium, a variant of this idea, was created by a team of researchers at Waseda University, Bell Labs, and Lancaster University. It uses a mirror-based display depicting swimming fish, and a toothbrush equipped with an accelerometer to determine if a user has brushed their teeth properly. The health of the fish is linked to the user's toothbrushing activity, keeping them strong with regular brushing, but weakening them if neglected. The motivation it produces is well documented, and it appears to be highly effective at incentivizing regular brushing, even among adults.[†]

[†] Nakajima, Tatsuo, and Fahim Kawsar. "Designing Ambient and Personalised Displays to Encourage Healthier Lifestyles." (*http://www.fahim-kawsar.net/papers/Nakajima.JAISE2012.Camera.pdf*)

This is an excellent example of a calm interaction because it uses a light-based or visual graphic notification instead of an annoying beeping sound, an email, a text message, or anything else excessively intrusive to remind you to brush your teeth. Much like a notification icon on a phone or a desktop, the device draws attention to itself in a quiet way. The fact that you'll only see it in the room where you would actually use the toothbrush is an example of smart contextual notification.

The color of the light is important here: red feels anxious, while a blue light is more of a gentle reminder. It's also a self-sufficient device. Because it uses an internal timed sensor, the toothbrush doesn't need to connect to an external network or application, or over Bluetooth. No application needs to be installed or updated, and no external device is necessary. The toothbrush works as a self-contained object that improves your behavior. Simple, right? It's also a good example of Principle VII: *The right amount of technology is the minimum needed to solve the problem.*

Self-inflating inhaler

For a different sort of visual indicator, consider the inhaler designed to be treated as a mechanical "pet" for kids requiring daily asthma medication. The inhaler puffs itself up with air so it is plump and full by morning, and the child is instructed to take care of their "pet" by deflating it, creating a gentle reminder to take their medication each morning. The relationship fostered is much like those between nano-pets and their owners.

STATUS TONES

Sound matters. Sound can put a user at ease or put them on edge during their interaction with a device, a website, or a piece of software. **A calm, welcoming sound can change everything about the experience,** and can relieve tension in frustrated users.

Far from being a simple on/off indicator, a well-designed status tone (much like a well-designed status light) can also serve as a unique identifier with relatively little cognitive demand. It allows technology to communicate information without using the spoken word, and without requiring the attention and distraction that verbal communication demands.

Getting this right means doing more with the tone than simply making an arbitrary sound, though. In many Japanese factories, for example, the alarm that stops the production line is actually a short tune that is customized to the team that sounds the alarm. This serves the dual function of letting the people on the floor know what's happening, and enforcing a sense of ownership among workers for the factory's process. It also lets everyone in the factory know, in seconds, where to start looking for problems to fix.

The Difference a Sound Makes

The startup tone on Apple computers is a prime example of a status tone that signals a transition in a calming way—though it was not always so. The boot-up tone on early Mac desktops was very harsh. "When Apple first started up, the computer was far from perfect," explains Jim Reeks, an Apple sound designer, in a recent podcast on sound and product design. Reeks worked at Apple Computer from 1988–1999 and hated the startup sound that early Macs made:

> It crashed a lot…and every time you turned it back on, you heard that jolting sound… Your Mac just crashed. Again. You lost your work… Again. And then you boot up and you heard this horrible [startup] noise! I was thinking about a zen-like, meditating sound, similar to a gong, or a chanting ohm.*

The podcast goes on to explain that Reeks couldn't initially get permission to replace the old sound with his new one, so he snuck it into the prototype, counting on its obvious calming nature to win the rest of the team over. It has become the sound most associated with Apple—the brand's audio signifier.

---

* *All quotes from 99 Percent Invisible, Episode 148: The Sizzle, 2015. (http://99percentinvisible.org/episode/the-sizzle).*

Sometimes status tones are used to **add emphasis** to status lights, but in other cases they can stand on their own. Status tones often accompany visual indicators: the tone alerts the user to a status change and the status light remains on as a persistent indicator.

Status tones are often an excellent way to communicate information without disrupting the user, but as with any indicator, it takes care to design them to be both effective and calm. A well-designed tone is engineered to be heard above other sounds (including those in the user's anticipated environment), but not to be something that jars the user out of their environment. Leave that to the more urgent status shout, covered in an upcoming section.

While there are no hard-and-fast rules for designing good status tones, there are general patterns, and an abundance of examples. What follows is a list of effective and calming status tones, both familiar and exploratory, along with some key considerations that went into making them right:

Help button on a plane
> When a passenger presses the overhead help button on an airplane, a status tone fires, alerting the flight attendants that someone needs attention. But more than that, a secondary system of status lights tells the flight attendants where the passenger is located on the plane. By letting person A create an alert for person B, then persisting until person B turns it off, the technology itself facilitates a person-to-person interaction in the least intrusive way possible.

Washer or dryer with a melody
> Have you ever encountered a washer or dryer that buzzes loudly when finished? While designed to catch the attention of someone elsewhere in the house, this kind of noise can often be interruptive and irritating. To counter this, some washers and dryers employ melodies when they're finished. A new line of Samsung washing machines play a short tune when the cycle is done. Other washing machines emit a quiet but positive tone when they are opened; the sound of an appliance excited to do its task. For many people living or working alone, these simple, bright tones subtly improve the mood and create a positive association with an otherwise unloved chore. Regardless, getting the volume right is very important. If you're not sure where the machine might be used, allowing the volume to be adjusted can be a wise idea.

Insulin pump

An insulin pump beeps when the user needs medication, but in a relatively quiet way that its wearer can deal with. It's not a particularly welcome device, but a necessary evil, and something many diabetics must deal with every day. As a wearer, you need to be alerted that it's time to attend to your insulin and blood sugar levels, but you also don't want the alert to intrude into your personal interactions. Getting this balance right has been a major contributor to the embrace of insulin monitors and pumps‡ among the community.

Roomba vacuum cleaner

The Roomba is a dinner-plate-sized disk of electronics that operates robotically to clean your floor. It chirps happily when a task is finished. When it gets stuck or needs cleaning, it emits a distinct somber tone. Orange and green status lights serve as secondary displays to confirm the situation, so if you missed the tone, you can still access the information in a different, low-impact way. The Roomba is an approachable piece of technology because it doesn't try to decide something on behalf of the user—when it gets stuck it asks for help.

HAPTIC ALERTS

Haptic alerts are physical notifications that can be felt on the body. The most common uses for haptic alerts today are for users of smartphones and other portable devices who want to receive notifications *without alerting other people* or intruding on social interactions. There's also a secondary use case where haptic feedback is used in conjunction with audio or visual feedback to add richness and detail, most commonly in video gaming. In general, haptic feedback is heavily driven by context, and often feels very personal and visceral. More than any other form of digital communication, it's something you "feel in your gut."

Relative to visual and audio, haptic notification is an underutilized channel, both in its frequency and in the amount of detail it communicates. More than hearing, **human touch is extremely high resolution**, with an extraordinary range of sensitivity, **yet for the most part we use haptic signals as one-bit notifications:** on or off, message present or

---

‡ "My father can't hear his Medtronic Pump." Insulin Pump Forums, 2010. (*http://www.insulinpumpforums.com/lofiversion/index.php?t3809.html*)

absent. Some of the most exciting research in human–computer interaction over the past decade focuses on better ways to harness haptic bandwidth, but designers have generally been slow to embrace it.

Haptics aren't just a single kind of buzz, but a wide range of sensations that can be utilized to get a message across. People are capable of rapidly learning different alert patterns, from Morse code to the buzz on a phone to the feedback from a game controller. Calm Technology requires that we pass the least amount of information necessary to get the point across to the user, in order to respect their limited attention. Better facility with haptic notification, and an understanding of when it's appropriate to use, is a major step forward in product design.

Here are some current and potential examples of the use of haptic alerts:

Feedback from a video game controller
> Video game controllers with haptic feedback can help the player feel more immersed in a game while retaining focus, without adding to the already oversaturated visual and auditory cues and feedback in the game. Sensing this feedback can help players make decisions and grow in the game without deviating or getting distracted from the sounds and visuals that are already there. Haptic feedback on the controller is a secondary or tertiary notification, leaving the visual field wide open so users can focus on gameplay as the primary task.

Buzz on a smartphone
> The most basic kind of haptic alert: "something has happened!" Lately we're seeing the first nods toward increasing the resolution of smartphone buzzes, with different patterns for texts, updates, and phone calls, but these are still poorly differentiated and inconsistent.

Smartwatch alert
> A smartwatch is an example of bringing information closer to you. That information may cause you to take a closer look and respond through your smartphone, or it may just be passing a message ("the lights in your house are on" or "Sarah arrived home safely," or something more personal like "you're nearing an area where others have reported an asthma attack" or "it's getting late and you need to eat"). Getting such notifications from a

watch often makes more sense than getting them from a smartphone, as there's less chance of getting distracted by the bombardment of news, alerts, and social communication that comes with opening a smartphone interface.

AMBER alert or emergency alert

As people move away from radio, television, and landline telephones, there needs to be a way to send emergency alerts. An AMBER alert on a smartphone, indicated by a unique tone and vibration, overrides other modes and grabs your attention. However, there are bandwidth limitations to sending emergency alerts out to every phone in a given area. A better system is a physical alert system based on an area, as it's loud enough for most people in the affected range to hear.

LUMOBack posture sensor

The LUMOBack sensor is a device worn around the waist that notices and detects changes in posture. When you exhibit good posture, the sensor does nothing. But as soon as you begin to slouch, the device buzzes on your back. The buzz makes you aware of your posture using the sense of touch. There is no display, and no audio tone. This is a perfect example of a Calm Technology using a different kind of sense to signal a problem. The device is calm because it only alerts you when you need to change your behavior (the slouch), and because it uses your sense of touch, you don't run the risk of alerting others (with a sound notification) or becoming visually distracted (in the case of a visual notification). It is a perfect example of Calm Technology. It is silent until it needs to message you. It fulfills the intention of alerting you when your posture is poor.

Turn-by-turn directions

Have you ever turned on the GPS in your car and then tried to have a conversation? The auditory and visual nature of turn-by-turn directions tends to put conversation, along with many other aspects of daily life, on hold. Walking down the street holding a phone in front of your face, for example, is a terrible way to experience the world around you.

Haptic feedback offers the possibility of compressing turn-by-turn directions into a series of buzzes. Two buzzes for left, one buzz for right, for example, with variations in intensity as the turn approaches—a kind of Morse code for everyday life. If done well, this would lift the demand on the user to look at a screen or listen to audio instructions, allowing us to drive, talk, walk, and experience life with our eyes and ears, yet still get the same resolution of data (or possibly an even higher level). In some cases, this might be safer, too, as it would cause less distraction than looking at directions (say, when driving a car).

In a paper called "A Tactile Compass for Eyes-free Pedestrian Navigation,"[§] researchers described an experiment involving a belt that persistently buzzed in the direction of north, worn non-stop by participants for six weeks. At the end of the study, one researcher recalled having a "6th sense of direction," including the ability to feel the buzz of direction while he explored landscapes during nighttime dreams.[¶]

In a more concrete development, both Apple and Google began integrating haptics into their direction systems in 2014 and 2015. Apple created haptic feedback for turn-by-turn walking directions with the Apple Watch and Apple Maps.[**] Google allows the same thing through Google Maps.

STATUS SHOUTS

Status shouts are reserved for very important or time-sensitive information: smoke alarms, fire alarms, teakettles, microwaves, and the like. Status shouts tend to use audio cues, but we could imagine visual and haptic status shouts as well.

[§] Pielot, Martin, Benjamin Poppinga, Wilko Heuten, Jeschua Schang, and Susanne Boll. "A Tactile Compass for Eyes-free Pedestrian Navigation," 2011. (*http://pielot.org/wp-content/uploads/2011/05/Pielot2011-TactileCompass.pdf*)

[¶] feelSpace: Report of a Study Project. (May 2005) Universität Osnabrück. Institute of Cognitive Science Department of Neurobiopsychology. Retrieved April 22, 2011. (*http://cogsci.uni-osnabrueck.de/~feelspace/downloads/feelSpace_finalReport.pdf*)

[**] "Apple Watch's Walking Directions Buzz Your Wrist When It's Time to Turn." Gizmodo, 2014. (*http://gizmodo.com/apple-watch-will-give-you-a-buzz-when-its-time-to-turn-1632557384*)

One major edge case to consider with audio status shouts is that they will be useless to those without hearing. Could visual or haptic status shouts be a solution to this edge case with the technology of the future? Perhaps.

Imagine a world in which we installed solar roadways across the nation. What would it be like to have a visual status shout? We'd have a complete infrastructure that would have an alert state, and if you were anywhere outside you'd be able to see it. All of the roads lit up would be a status shout. Blue or green. And they could light the direction to take to reach the higher ground.

LED city lights could also be addressable to convey status shouts and emergency indicators. We could wire the system into buildings to provide warning lights for evacuations in the event of an earthquake or other emergency.

What about haptic shouts? If everyone had a strong **emergency vibration** as a feature on mobile phones, you could send a direct signal that can't easily be ignored to every phone at once. This could be a more successful way of transmitting emergency alerts through mobile technology than the current method of using text messages, whose notifications can be silenced or easily missed—text messages do not shout. We could even use notifications on what is available in the home: Nest thermostats, or in a business, connected Square cash registers.

Ambulances use status shouts to alert those around them to make way for an emergency. Tornado warnings shout: "Take cover!" **A good status shout is unambiguous.** You would never mistake the shrill tone of a teakettle for your toaster oven; both tones are loud, but one shrieks and the other dings. These signals tell you something is complete, or, in the case of a smoke detector, that something is **wrong**!

When designing a status shout, first ask if the information you need to get across is truly urgent. Does it indicate something life threatening? Does it demand an immediate response, or a change in tempo of everyone near? An emergency vehicle's siren can be heard for many blocks before it arrives, and so gives people time to get out of the way. Alerts from a washer or dryer can be heard from across the home. A loud status shout in the form of a song works well. Consider the frequency of the alert: **the more frequent the alert, the calmer it should be.** If the information comes up multiple times a day or even a couple of times a week, the signal may need calming down, or the repeated jarring may cause the user anxiety or even prompt them to turn it off.

Here are some examples of status shouts:

Seat belt on/off alert

Instead of simply showing a visual indicator of whether the seat belt is being used or not, many cars emit an annoying ringing or beeping noise if weight is felt on the seat and the seat belt is not engaged. This can cause problems if you have a package in the seat next to you, triggering the alert. However, it is effective—I've seen people instinctively grab the seatbelt and put it on when the tone rings, just to prevent the sound from continuing.

Smoke detector

The unambiguous tone of a smoke detector is so intense that it causes panic, and rightly so, as waking up in time could be a literal case of life or death. But smoke alarms are also a good example of the potentially disastrous consequences of false alarms. Before the mid-1980s, one of the few ways to deal with a smoke alarm that kept going off when there was no danger (while cooking, for example) was to remove its batteries. The problem, of course, is that it's easy to forget to put the batteries back in, and a smoke detector doesn't work without batteries. In many cases, this is still a problem today, and when fires go undetected, people die.

Coleman, a company better known for camping equipment, engaged a design agency called Ziba[††] to redesign its smoke detectors, and they came up with the idea of a large round button that could temporarily silence the alarm. Dubbed the "broom button," it was intentionally designed to be easy to hit with a broom handle. This feature proved so popular that Coleman quickly took 40% of the smoke detector market, and the broom button became industry standard within a few years. Coleman's new line also offered a variety of detectors for different rooms: more sensitive ones for bedrooms, detectors with built-in lighting for hallways, and detectors with adjustable sensitivity for kitchens. The ultimate result was

---

[††] Coleman Safe Keep Smoke Detector. Ziba, date unknown. (*http://www.ziba.com/work/coleman-safe-keep-smoke-detector*)

greater market share for Coleman and greater safety for users—paradoxically, by making it easier to *prevent* the detector from "doing its job."

The lesson for designers is clear: when creating a status shout, pay special attention to false positives, and make sure there's a way to shut them off easily, make them less intrusive, or avoid them in the first place.

Parking garage warning buzzer

Parking garages in urban areas often emit a loud buzz when a vehicle exits onto the street to warn pedestrians and passing drivers of the approaching car. For passing drivers, though, this has lately started to cause problems, as many modern cars now come with audible proximity alerts. When the insistent beeping of an internal proximity alert sounds at the same time as an external garage buzzer, the response can be panic and confusion, ultimately making the situation less safe than if there'd been no alarm at all.

When designing status shouts, look for potential conflicts with other status shouts in the user's environment, and design to accommodate them, or at least to avoid negating them.

Emergency vehicle truck siren

Police cars, ambulances, and fire trucks are unusual vehicles that announce their presence with equally unusual audio indicators. Their sirens serve several purposes. They draw attention to the vehicle, and to the unusual and potentially dangerous situation they're responding to. They change the tempo of surrounding traffic. They also have the direct function of convincing other vehicles to slow down and pull to the side of the street, allowing the shouting vehicle to get to its urgent task more quickly.

All status shouts change the behavior of the people who hear them. It's important to design the shout in a way that encourages the most constructive behavior.

Recess bell

Loud status shouts don't always need to signal negative things. The recess bell is one example of a positive status shout—a loud, unambiguous signal that notifies teachers and students that it's time for play and socializing. In a similar way, the alarms that sound the end of a class or work shift, or the start of a lunch break, are status shouts that are designed to be intrusive, but also positive. They drown out all other activity because they're supposed to drown it out, and in so doing convey an organizational belief that break time is important enough to demand its own attention.

Ambient Awareness

Consider your space of awareness. In front of you is high-resolution perception; as you go into your peripheral vision, you can still see and sense color, but you can't necessarily make out the details of an item. **Ambient awareness means making use of the peripheral environment**, whether it is a visual display outside of the center field of view, a subtle tone, or a vibration nearby that allows you to know something without needing to look. Ambient awareness means **a notification is present by default: opt out, rather than opt in.**

For much of our evolution, we received information directly from other humans and the environment. **Our experience of receiving messages and information was tactile and rich with sensory information.** It was also rich with human information—body language, status, and emotional tone, but also the briefest of emotive expressions. **Our brains are uniquely evolved to attend to and comprehend this type of information** and pay attention to the most important parts. We have changed our environment through technology, and we need to learn to refit our environment to us.

We've discussed how important it is to make use of peripheral attention in order to avoid overwhelming the user, and ambient awareness is a tool for doing exactly that. The terms "peripheral attention" and "ambient awareness" can be used interchangeably. Ambient awareness is not a *different kind* of notification; **it is a principle that says, when possible, load things into the environment** so that all of the attention doesn't need to be constantly checking for a state change. This is essentially a restatement of Principle III (make use of the periphery) in different language.

"Peripheral attention" was the term used by Weiser and Brown, but "ambient awareness" seems to connote a very broad environment to affect through the use of design, and brings a sense of fuzzy emotional well-being with it, which is perhaps why this term has been more commonly used in recent years.

The key to ambient awareness is not to overwhelm. If you're using a beacon or information emitter to create ambient awareness, consider the environment around it. The size and location of the beacon is important. Logic and intuition are required to choose where your notifications go. Should you put it in the user's peripheral vision? At eye level? Is haptic information *automatically* ambient? (It is if it's persistently buzzing, but not if it only buzzes you in single bursts as an alert.) Something too large could distract, and something too small could be overlooked. It is important to test your approach to see if your users can tell what's happening without removing their attention from the primary task at hand.

It's worth looking at two of Weiser and Brown's favorite examples, the inner office window and an interactive art project called "Live Wire"— they are ideal illustrations of the fundamental concept of placing information openly and usefully in the ambient environment. Both do a masterful job of conveying crucial information without adding unnecessarily to the user's cognitive load.

In "The Coming Age of Calm Technology," Weiser and Brown write that the inner office window (Figure 3-2) **extends our periphery** by creating a two-way channel for clues about the environment. A person can easily see whether someone is busy or not without having to interrupt them. By providing exactly the right amount of visibility, an inner window actually **reduces the amount of attention required to satisfy an informational need:**

> Whether it is motion of other people down the hall (it's time for a lunch; the big meeting is starting), or noticing the same person peeking in for the third time while you are on the phone (they really want to see me; I forgot an appointment), the (inner office) window connects the person inside to the nearby world.

FIGURE 3-2
The inner office window.

The Live Wire‡‡ (Figure 3-3) was an 8-foot piece of plastic spaghetti created by artist Natalie Jeremijenko. It hung from a small electric motor mounted in the ceiling outside the door to Mark Weiser's office. As Weiser and Brown describe in "Designing Calm Technology," the motor was electrically connected to a nearby Ethernet cable, and wired "so that each bit of information that goes past causes a tiny twitch of the motor. A very busy network causes a madly whirling string with a characteristic noise; a quiet network causes only a small twitch every few seconds." The Live Wire wasn't just an interesting piece of art. For many of the IT professionals at PARC, it was also quite useful. The long string was visible and audible without being obtrusive. The installation communicated enough detail about network traffic for the typical observer without the need to log into a computer terminal. As Weiser and Brown noted, the Live Wire "uses no software, only a few dollars in hardware, and can be shared by many people at the same time."§§

---

‡‡ Livewire, Natalie Jeremijenko, date unknown. (*http://tech90s.walkerart.org/nj/transcript/nj_04.html*)

§§ Weiser, Mark, and John Seely Brown. "Designing Calm Technology." Xerox PARC, December 21, 1995.

FIGURE 3-3

Live Wire: original 1995 installation of artist-in-residence Natalie Jeremijenko's Ethernet-connected interactive art piece. The installation hung outside Weiser's door at Xerox PARC.

Many notifications that take up valuable center-vision real estate are actually better **suited for this kind of treatment,** not just because it makes them less intrusive, but also because **it turns their presence into something reliable and comforting**, rather than an interruption to be dispensed with. Windows in a car, for instance, provide ambient awareness, and you don't turn them off during the entire drive. In fact, if they get blocked (by rain or snow), that's when you're in trouble. Under what circumstances does it make sense to have a light that is always on, or a sound that is always there unless something makes it go away? It may be calming to provide persistent sensory feedback to confirm that something is operating correctly, like a streetlamp that is always on, and only shuts off when broken. Likewise, knowing that something is "done" or "handled" in the background can gives users a sense of finality and closure; a feeling of satisfaction that something has been taken care of.

This is useful when you need to provide information to someone without interrupting their primary task. A soft light that changes color with the weather is one example; a globe that changes color based on the time of day is another. A gradual change in an ambient beacon or display can also draw attention to a more complex display or dashboard. In airplane cockpits, for example, ambient visual indicators often inform someone of a change, augmented by a status tone when additional attention is needed. Let's look at some other examples:

Lavatory occupied sign

The number one safety issue on a plane is not the plane crashing, but unsecured people being tossed about the cabin. An airplane is one of the most space-constrained environments one might ever be in, which makes it crucial to keep passengers from milling about the galley areas, checking the availability of the bathroom. Because of this, it's well worth the extra effort and cost to give a clear indication of when it is vacant and when it's in use, because that little bit of extra security keeps people in their seats, buckled in where they can't get hurt by turbulence.

The simple pictographic display is universal and requires no translation. There are two colors, but it's not even an issue if you're red/green color-blind—the bold X is enough to get the idea across. And even if you're not wearing your glasses or don't have very good vision, you can tell the lavatory is occupied just by casually glancing up.

Directional tape on a floor

I attended a conference in Rotterdam as part of the Interaction 2013 Conference. The Rotterdam Design Institute had colored tape on the floor leading attendees to specific rooms. The signs on the floor show directions: each color designates a path on the route to a different room, making the entire Institute navigable, even by newcomers.

Weather-colored lightbulb (conceptual)

The weather-colored light bulb, based on a prototype built by Aaron Parecki, shows the current weather through color, by connecting a three-color LED light bulb to the Internet and feeding the results of the weather report through custom software. The result is a far more calm experience than watching The Weather Channel or constantly checking an app. Bright yellow symbolizes a sunny day, gray stands for cloudy, light blue for rainy, and deep blue for very rainy. Additionally, an iPad mounted to the wall can display more weather information if the user is interested.

Ambient information through color can prevent users from getting inundated with external information, by deferring it to peripheral vision and offering the option of going to a related notification for greater detail. In a similar vein, Parecki also created an experimental data status light for other types of information that, like the weather, get checked frequently (e.g., bank account balances or server status). By boiling a complex information set down to just three levels—green for "OK," yellow for "concern," and red for "problem"—a simple glance at a light can take the place of the time-consuming task of logging in and checking, multiple times a day.

Email Garden (conceptual)

In the Email Garden¶¶, industrial designer Nick Rodrigues offers a synthetic landscape of grass-like fibers emerging through a plastic container. The installation is synchronized with the artist's email account, causing the grass-like fibers to "grow" at the rate of incoming mail. Over time, the desk transforms from a useful work surface into an overflowing vessel of synthetic communication and endless obligations. While not particularly practical, the Email Garden gives some sense of how tactile and visual ambient awareness can be used to add a dimension of playfulness to an otherwise completely functional task.

Contextual Notifications

Each status indicator or change in ambient awareness must be triggered by some external action. Having an understanding of contextual notifications and triggers allows you to see where they work well and where they don't work well in the world. We can define a *trigger* as the shift that causes a notification as a result of an event.

A trigger has a precondition, a notification state, and a post-condition. When setting up a trigger for a notification, figure out what the precondition or context for the trigger is, then determine what kind(s) of notifications work best, and finally, test your post-condition.

¶¶ Email Garden, Nick Rodrigues. (*http://www.nickrodrigues.com/paintings-1/email-garden*)

A *timed notification* is an alert that happens at a **set interval** or **predetermined time**, and often results in a status shout. An alarm clock is a simple timed trigger: set the alarm, and it will alert you to the time you set. The post-condition is that the alarm may be snoozed, canceled, left on, or unplugged entirely. Similarly, a kitchen timer can be set to a number of minutes or hours, and alerts you when that time has elapsed. School, work, and church bells are also set on timed schedules.

As a general rule, **notifications that are triggered in this way tend to feel mechanical, distant, and detached.** Here we have a device that we are setting or turning on, and at some point in the future, it screams at us. Movies and popular culture use the trope of the automated countdown timer to generate an air of anxiety and danger for just this reason.

When you are designing a contextual notification with a timed element, take special care to **make it easy to set, adjust, stop, or turn off.** The snooze button is usually the largest one on the alarm clock, so that it can easily be tapped when one wakes up. The alarm clock for the iPhone works the same way, but it takes a little more effort to get to the button. This is one reason why many people prefer mechanical kitchen timers over the clock on their stove: it's a discrete, easily manipulated object, which makes it less intimidating, and more calm.

The other kind of trigger is the *contextual trigger*. Status notifications often have contextual triggers; that is, they indicate that something has changed, or that a specific event has occurred. A contextual trigger can range from a notification that you've received a text message to a sensor in your car that beeps at you when you're too close to another car.

As soon as you set a trigger, you're putting yourself at the mercy of something that's happening outside of the system. You have to be aware that sometimes that external event might fail, could be corrupted, or might just not show up in the system in the first place. This is a failure case that is often overlooked by designers, yet is depressingly common on the side of the users.

One way that online forms have evolved is to let you know when they're missing a crucial field, rather than simply failing with no explanation. For every contextual trigger, there's a secondary trigger that kicks in if the primary one fails. It's much more calming to be led back to the point of failure than to be told a mysterious flaw has destroyed your workflow.

Make sure you have a backup system that gracefully degrades to the technology's original intent. The SleepCycle application is a contextual extension of an alarm clock. If it fails to track the external data of your sleep, it defaults to being an alarm clock. The app still wakes you up at the time you set, regardless of whether the external data upon which it depends is present.

Consider creating a status tone that increases in volume toward a shout if not attended to—some modern bedside alarms, like Sleep Cycle, use this approach (Figure 3-4).

The Sleep Cycle app graphs sleep over time, compressing long-term data into an easily accessible format. This allows users to track how external variables like caffeine, exercise, and alcohol impact sleep.

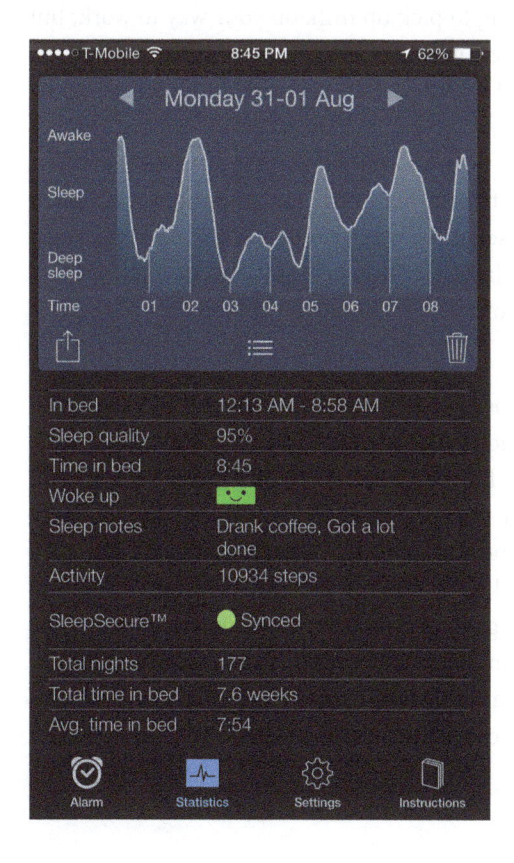

FIGURE 3-4

Sleep data from one night of sleep tracked by the Sleep Cycle application for iPhone—the application uses your movement while you sleep to determine the best time to wake you up in the morning in accordance with whether you are in deep sleep or in lighter REM sleep.

You can use particular contexts to set up interactions with technology. Some examples of contextual notifications in action come from weather, location, time, metabolic and emotional states, and proximity:

Weather

> If your device or application can read **temperature**, either itself or via an external service, you can message the user in interesting ways. For instance, Dark Sky is an application that uses a hyperlocal **weather** service to send a push **notification** to users when it is about to start or stop raining near them. This is especially helpful for people who commute by bike.

Location

> Using location allows you to set triggers that are based on being in a certain place at a certain time. For instance, when you drive past a grocery store anytime from 4 PM to 6 PM, you could get a reminder to pick up milk. This type of application is contextually aware that you're probably not going to pick up milk on your way to work, but you might forget to pick it up on your way home. Allowing the user to set the time and location of the reminder allows for a sense of control. Instead of getting many irrelevant notifications, understanding when the best time to send the message can be the difference between a product that is essential and one that is just plain annoying. Location-based alerts can also be used to inform people close to you when you land at the airport so they can pick you up, or inform the doctor's office that you've arrived on site.

Time

> Time is one of the most basic contextual triggers, but it can be used in blended situations. For instance, you could get a message when you need to leave for the airport based on current traffic conditions, or get an alert that you need to leave for a meeting with the walking distance and a map built in. More basic alerts can be a phone call that is timed to get you out of a meeting, or a lamp that dims when it is time to go to bed. The application Flux changes the color of the light on your computer screen when it gets to be nighttime, preventing insomnia by allowing the circadian rhythm and melatonin production to kick in.

Emotional and metabolic state

Triggers might be helpful when you need to be notified of a medical or physiological need, such as low blood sugar or the need to take a nap or take insulin. Some applications might monitor activity through the user's phone and reach out to a network of predetermined friends if changes in usage patterns are detected. The Compass app for iPhone tracked how users were spending their day. If there wasn't much movement, the app could notify friends to check in with them to make sure they were OK. Google's smart contact lens,*** announced in 2014, is a project aimed at helping people with diabetes by constantly measuring glucose levels in tears via a wireless chip and a miniaturized glucose sensor integrated in the lens.

Proximity

Proximity can be used to notify someone if there are interesting people nearby. The former mobile application Meet Gatsby used location-based check-in data from popular application Foursquare to provide a virtual concierge that introduced users to people near their current location that shared interests, based on a few simple questions. From 2010–2013, location-based application company Geoloqi provided a location-based notification application that brought to life public datasets and nearby points of interest such as geocoded Wikipedia articles and pinball machines. Users were able to leave "Geonotes" for themselves and others, allowing people to serendipitously encounter interesting information about the world around them, such as blackberry bushes nearby or the start of a bike ride.

Accomplishment

Contextual notifications can also provide rewards for movement. For instance, the Nike+ step tracker wristband buzzes and lights up, creating a feeling of accomplishment and celebration for users who met their daily exercise goal.

*** "Introducing our smart contact lens project," Google Official Blog, 2014. (*https:// googleblog.blogspot.fr/2014/01/introducing-our-smart-contact-lens.html*)

Persuasive Technology

Persuasive technologies are technologies that change what we think and do. In 1996 scientist B.J. Fogg created the term "captology" to describe the study of computers as persuasive technologies (captology comes from the acronym Computers As Persuasive Technologies)." In 2003, Fogg published *Persuasive Technology: Using Computers to Change What We Think and Do*. He is now the director of the Persuasive Technology Lab at Stanford University.

Persuasive technology doesn't have to impact the user directly. It can also motivate their network of friends or community to check in with them. Or recall the bitter solution to nail biting earlier in this chapter. Sometimes a bad taste can deter you from doing something bad for you.

A good persuasive technology largely depends on taking what was formerly invisible (behaviors, decisions, unseen consequences) **and making it visible**. Crucial to making this work is making data collection as low-friction as possible. The less effort users must put into recording or submitting data, the more insight they'll be able to gain.

Unfortunately, many feedback loops in our environment are "dark" user experiences or "user interfaces designed to trick people":[†††] they get us to buy things we do not want, and feel bad if we leave the store without a fresh item, or walk down the street without the right style of clothing on. Because of these influences, instead of being calm, focused, and creative, we feel increasingly anxious.

Even though some of our experiences on the modern Web could be considered dark user experiences, positive persuasive technologies could be very useful for a wide range of our modern problems, from energy consumption to healthy mental states; from connecting us to others to making the most of one's time. There is so much potential and so much work to be done here to improve and enhance the lives of people. If we spent the last half of the 20th century working on systems to take up more of people's time, the next century might find us creating or removing technologies—to many of us, a more positive experience.

[†††] See "Dark Patterns: fighting user deception worldwide," 2015. (*http://darkpatterns.org*)

Here are a few examples of persuasive technologies at work:

Alpha wave synchrony feedback machine

This system connects to brainwave-monitoring electrodes that trigger a tone when you get into a harmonious pattern of brainwaves. Dubbed "alpha synchrony," these kinds of waves have been associated with feelings of calmness and alertness.[‡‡‡] Practicing this method of "technologically guided meditation" measurably improves the user's ability to reach and maintain specific brain states. Alpha wave synchrony feedback is an example of how incredibly effective feedback loops can be, not only at the surface level but beyond. An electroencephalogram (EEG) makes your (formerly invisible) brainwaves visible and opens up the possibility to alter how we think in dramatic ways. Biofeedback training can slow down heart rate and increase blood flow to certain areas. Neurofeedback can even train epileptics to prevent themselves from going into seizures when they have adequate warning.

GlowCap

GlowCap (*http://www.vitality.net/glowcaps.html*) is light-embedded cap that can be attached to the top of a standard pill bottle. The cap glows when it is time for a patient to take their medication. Multiple colors allow the device to indicate which pill to take at which time, and the light stays on until the cap is unscrewed.

This kind of status indicator uses a very simple, subtle visual cue to help patients with prescription compliance, a long-standing problem in medicine. In a small study, the manufacturers reportedly found[§§§] that the GlowCap increased a person's likelihood of taking their medication on time to 86%: "a figure that is 'astounding' in the field of persuasive tech," according to Stanford Persuasive Technology Lab founder B.J. Fogg. Studies

---

[‡‡‡] Recent scientific research links alpha waves to "neural structures underpinning control of alertness and task requirements." Source: Sadaghiani, Sepideh, René Scheeringa, Katia Lehongre, Benjamin Morillon, Anne-Lise Giraud, Mark D'Esposito, and Andreas Kleinschmidt. "Alpha-Band Phase Synchrony Is Related to Activity in the Fronto-Parietal Adaptive Control Network." *The Journal of Neuroscience* 32, no. 41 (2012): 14305-4310.

[§§§] "Tech guilt: 5 'persuasive' technologies to help you be good." CNN Tech, 2010. (*http://www.cnn.com/2010/TECH/innovation/08/13/guilt.gadgets*)

have shown that approximately "half of all patients do not take their medications as prescribed,"[¶¶¶] and "adherence is lowest among patients with chronic illnesses."[****]

OPOWER

At times, comparing one's behavior to that of others can act as a deterrent or incentive. For instance, home energy company OPOWER collects energy data from customers' homes and displays it in a chart that compares their energy use to that of their neighbors, providing positive reinforcement for those who use relatively less energy by labeling their energy-consumption readouts with a smiley face. OPOWER reportedly claims[††††] that "Such exposure causes 60 to 80 percent of people to change their energy behaviors." According to a company spokesman, "If we could take this nationwide—and there's no reason why we can't—we can take 3 million homes off the grid and have as much impact as the entire renewable [energy] sector."

Withings scale

The Withings Smart Body Analyzer (*http://www.withings.com/eu/en/products/smart-body-analyzer*) is a small wireless scale that tracks your weight over time and allows you to see a graph of your progress on your smartphone (though seeing the graph on the scale itself would be a useful addition). The resulting feedback loop can help people scale up their exercise or scale back on their eating to maintain a healthy weight. It is often useful for seeing how longer-term trends such as significant life events can affect weight.

Toyota Prius driver feedback

When Toyota released a vehicle with a real-time driver feedback system, the change in driver behavior became known as the "Prius Effect." The Prius dashboard displays feedback on the driver's behavior, identifying coasting, acceleration, braking, and cruising.

[¶¶¶] Sokol, Michael C., Kimberly A. McGuigan, Robert R. Verbrugge, and Robert S. Epstein. "Impact of Medication Adherence on Hospitalization Risk and Healthcare Cost." *Medical Care* 43, no. 6 (2005): 521-30.

[****] Osterberg, L., and T. Blaschke. "Adherence to Medication." *N Engl J Med* 353, no. 5 (2005): 487-97.

[††††] "Tech guilt: 5 'persuasive' technologies to help you be good." CNN Tech, 2010. (*http://www.cnn.com/2010/TECH/innovation/08/13/guilt.gadgets*)

These variables are displayed next to their effect on gas mileage. User experience researchers have explained that the position of the dashboard "near the driver's view of the road," with a current estimation of miles per gallon, has an impact on driver behavior[‡‡‡‡] that far outstrips the most effective education campaign.

Some smart cars have made the idea one step more abstract, by including in the display an image of a tree that grows when you drive efficiently, and dies when you don't.

Salad bar tongs

How do you give people feedback on what they're eating without distracting them from getting to their meal? Nashville-based Healthways Inc. placed colored salad bar tongs in their corporate lunchroom. The tongs were colored based on whether the food was considered healthy or not: green for healthy, yellow for moderate, and red for bad. Crumbled bacon would have red tongs, for instance, and the tongs for salad greens would be green.

This is a better choice than simply putting up "eat healthy" posters or posting nutritional information on every item, because it gives people feedback on their food choices at the moment of choice. This may create an environment where healthier choices can easily be made, simply by switching tongs.

Beeminder

A web service called Beeminder (*https://www.beeminder.com*) allows you to track your goals and attach financial consequences to negative outcomes. Say you'd like to quit smoking. You sign up with the service and state your goal, then provide it with your bank account details. When you go off track, the service takes your money. The system logarithmically increases the payment to increase the sting. This is clearly a system where you don't want to slack!

[‡‡‡‡] "Information Displays That Change Driver Behavior." UXMatters, 2014. (*http://www.uxmatters.com/mt/archives/2014/07/information-displays-that-change-driver-behavior.php*)

Conclusions

Calm Technology depends heavily on using notifications, triggers, ambient awareness, and persuasive technology in a more sensitive way—but **those elements do not, by themselves, automatically create a calm experience.**

In many cases, a simple tone or light can convey the same amount of information as a full display or pop-up box, while being much less distracting. The underlying concept is to match the resolution of the notification with the amount and importance of information being conveyed. Learn this, and the specific applications become obvious.

By far the most utilized sense for technological notification is vision, which is why it is also the most cluttered. This chapter points out the many different senses you can employ to compress information instead of "causing" more visual clutter. Designing for calm interaction is largely a matter of finding nonvisual ways to communicate low-priority information.

But underlying all of this is a question that very few designers ask themselves seriously: whether a notification is even necessary. There is a time, place, and context for notifications, and the trick to smooth computing is to work with your users to determine what is appropriate, helpful, and not distracting or anxiety producing. Just as we can get into trouble by creating a notification for everything that a device or piece of software does, we can also err by giving too few notifications. Calm Technology does not automatically mean sparse communication; it means **exactly the right amount of communication**—not for the technology's ability, but **for the user's needs.**

Alerts are usually hierarchical. Make a habit of testing everything you do in the real world to determine a hierarchy of information. Consider the primary focus of someone using your application or product, and ask yourself if any individual alert—like an emergency alert—is so important that it should remove the user from their current task.

If so, consider structuring the alert so that it supports, rather than detracts from, the primary task. Cars, for example, are designed to give numerous alerts that enhance the driver's ability to drive, such as a clicking turn signal indicator or a tachometer that moves into the red zone when your engine revs too high.

The next chapter presents exercises designed to help you apply the principles of Calm Technology from the previous chapter and the calm communication patterns covered in this one. We'll use a Calm Technology evaluation tool to better understand how objects interact with their environments.

Key takeaways from this chapter:

- Calm communication patterns can help to "calm down" an otherwise overly demanding interaction or interface.
- Try to pay more attention to status lights in your environment. Where do they come from? What do they indicate?
- The timing of a status tone is important, as is how you experience it. A calm, welcoming sound can relieve tension in frustrated users even when inconveniently timed.
- When designing a status shout, first ask if the information you need to get across is truly urgent.
- Ambient awareness means a notification is present by default: opt out, rather than opt in. What aspects of your environment could communicate information ambiently?
- A good persuasive technology largely depends on taking what was formerly invisible (behaviors, decisions, unseen consequences) and making it visible. What invisible information would be helpful if it were to be visible?
- Consider how you could use external changes to trigger contextual notifications through each of the status indicators.
- What devices in your life could be improved by changing their communication style, and why?

[4]

Exercises in Calm Technology

[NOTE]

For the latest version of these exercises, see *http://calmtech.com/exercises*.

To BEGIN WITH, WE'RE going to assume that most of the situations where you will be tasked with applying Calm Design principles will be ones that involve modifying existing interactions, rather than creating new ones. This recognizes the reality that technology gets created through improvement and iteration far more often than through disruption. Even in the case of a genuinely new device, service, or piece of software, the new is often still based on well-established standards. If you're making a smart light bulb, you still need to base it on existing light bulbs. Otherwise, it won't fit into the current ecosystem of related devices. More importantly, people won't know how to use it. You can't expect to change behavior unless you build on what people already know, so you will have to know how to make a connection from current technology to your innovation in the minds of users.

For designers seeking to make interactions with technology more "calm," this means expanding the idea of when a design task is "done." Frequently, when technology isn't calm, it's not because of any intentional decision about notifications and alerts, but because of a lack of intent—**we often think of a design as "complete" when it fulfills all of its functions, and leave the details of how it communicates to the user as an afterthought.** This is a ubiquitous problem in the world of design.

For this reason, this chapter opens with an evaluative tool, not a generative one. The tool is a straightforward method of analyzing the various states and interactions of a piece of technology in order to identify moments of unnecessary intrusion, and opportunities for calming them down.

Like many evaluative tools, its greatest value is simply in forcing us to look carefully at what we've created, and to consider the impact of that creation on someone who must live with it every day. It's an empathy-building tool, and in the process of building that empathy, solutions tend to appear, almost unbidden. It's also a powerful tool for explaining how a product works to managers and other team members, which can help developers as they work together to implement the design.

A Calm Interaction Evaluation Tool

At this point, we've already discussed the importance of having a framework or tool with which to organize your thoughts and understanding of an object and its ability to capture your attention. Table 4-1 shows you four questions to think about when designing or evaluating an object. The table is organized into three main sections:

User

How does the object interact with a person, and how does the product affect the user? How does the device catch your attention?

Environment

Where is the object in the real world? What other products might interact or conflict with the product's function or alert style? How does the product interact with the surrounding environment? This includes its physical environment (a kitchen, an office, etc.) as well as the most common actions of the user around the time when they are using it.

This category is important because it gives you details on whether the device itself is an issue, or whether the environment itself is an issue. **Connected devices have two components: the device itself and the environment in which it is placed.** Designers have to make predictions about the environment, but don't often have control over it.

For instance, you might make a device for use in the kitchen that works well with a calm status tone, but it might not be heard over the air conditioner in the window. In this case, it would be important to have a variable setting for tone, or an additional a non-auditory way of displaying the information.

Information
> What kind of information does the object provide, how is it stored, and what happens when information is missing?

Within each of these categories, you are asked to consider the effects of context, alert style, usage, and edge cases.

TABLE 4-1. Calm Technology evaluation tool

USER			
Context: What kind of person uses this device? What are their needs and their limitations?	**Alert Style:** What alert style does the object use to communicate? Does the alert demand all of your focus or just some of it?	**Usage:** What actions are required of the user to set up the device? How does the user turn off or acknowledge each alert?	**Edge Cases:** What kinds of people might have difficulties using the device?

ENVIRONMENT			
Context: Where does the device live? Is it a loud environment or a quiet one? Is it used in a home, an office, a factory, or outside (or some combination of these)? What exists in the environment that this object will have to interact with?	**Alert Style:** What in the environment could get in the way of the alert? At what times would an alert be inappropriate? Might the alert style need to change if the object is moved from environment to environment?	**Usage:** Does the environment place any limitations on the user's actions? (For example, users are somewhat restricted if they're wearing gloves, if they're in a public setting trying to use voice activation, etc.)	**Edge Cases:** What unusual environmental situations could render these alerts ineffective? How does the device deal with that?

INFORMATION			
Context: What do you need to know in order to use the object?	**Alert Style:** Does the attention the alert demands match the importance of the information the alert is communicating? What other options exist for communicating the same information?	**Usage:** What will the user do with the information they get from the device?	**Edge Cases:** What happens if the information is wrong or not present? How does the object let the person know that it needs assistance? Does it default to a previous analog state?

This Calm Technology evaluation tool can help you consider how technology fits into a person's life through their own interactions with it, the device's interaction with its environment, and how it communicates and makes use of information.

To use it, you could make copies of this page. Print out the chart or draw it on a whiteboard, or use Post-it notes on a wall. Just make sure these categories are represented. The idea is not to get it right the first time, but to use the tool for understanding the object and how it interacts with you and the myriad end users in all their variety.

This is not the be-all, end-all of evaluation tools, of course—it's probably too in-depth for some very simple pieces of technology, and obviously just scratching the surface for a multifunctional, layered device like a smartwatch. This is first and foremost a tool designed to help you do the exercises in this book. If you find it useful here, you may find it useful as a tool for product design. Within the context of these exercises, it's a way of getting you in the habit of looking closely at an object, and considering the ways in which it takes up attention or doesn't.

The Calm Technology evaluation tool is a kind of multiplication table for how a product can work. If you don't consider all of the outcomes in the chart, you may fail to identify something that could end up being crucial to a good experience.

Table 4-2 shows the Calm Technology evaluation tool filled out for the Philips Hue lighting system. It describes how the Hue system interacts with the human environment in terms of people, environmental factors, and information. Completing the evaluation tool can help to really understand the product.

TABLE 4-2. Evaluating the Philips Hue lighting system

USER			
Context: Hue lights are used primarily by people at home to turn their lights on and off by mobile phone, and to change the color of the lights in their environment.	**Alert Style:** The Hue alert style is a status light: on or off, with the addition of programmable, adjustable color. Hue light bulbs are accessed via a smartphone app that connects to the Hue hub. Lights are switched on and off through the app.	**Usage:** Users connect the Hue light bulbs to a Hue hub and connect the hub to a wireless network.	**Edge Cases:** People who are blind would need to use the physical switch provided by Hue or the light switch in the house to turn the lights on and off. People without a smartphone wouldn't be able to control the lights using the app.

ENVIRONMENT			
Context: The device lives at home, or sometimes at work. Existing light bulbs and light switches are in the environment and can be replaced by the Hue system.	**Alert Style:** The Hue would only become annoying if the light could not be changed or were stuck on a strange color.	**Usage:** The environment requires either the pressing of a Hue switch or having your phone near you to control the lights via an app. Devices like Amazon's Alexa can help by providing voice-command functionality.	**Edge Cases:** The power could go out, or the light color could be wrong, or the system could crash. Hue sometimes has issues loading the color hot pink. The device deals with it with a small delay.

INFORMATION			
Context: You need to be able to plug in the Hue hub, pair the system to your phone, and install the Hue light bulbs. Once you do that, you can access the lights from your phone.	**Alert Style:** The status light matches the user's intent and input.	**Usage:** The user will simply experience the light as it changes, or will decide to change the color of the light.	**Edge Cases:** Because the Hue system works on a network, it has gone down before. Hue officials on Twitter mentioned that people could use their light switches to turn the lights off. This is elegant, if known, because when the system is broken it defaults to previous social behavior.

Exercises

The easiest way to pursue these exercises is on your own, sitting at a desk, with your favorite writing and sketching tools in front of you, and maybe some music on. This is how a lot of design work gets done, after all, and it's probably an environment that's relatively easy to set up. If you decide to go solo, there are some possible solutions to each exercise posted at *http://calmtech.com/exercises* for you to compare with your own.

If you often work with a team, it may be useful to complete these exercises in a small group. The challenges and process are largely the same, though you'll also want to set aside some additional time to brainstorm concepts, then discuss and edit down to the most promising ones. It may also be useful to have each team member pursue a different solution, then compare your results at the end.

EXERCISE 1: A CALMER ALARM CLOCK

The interaction flow for most alarm clocks is fairly consistent and predictable: activate the alarm, set the wake time, receive a status shout at the specified time, hit the snooze button. Most are operated via digital push button, or occasionally rotational knob, but beyond that there's not a lot of variation. This exercise calls that consistency into question, and challenges you to improve on this simple design.

Consider the various switches and features of a standard alarm clock, as shown in Figure 4-3:

Front face
1. Status display (always shows the time; lit by LED)
2. AM/PM indicator (light turns on if it is PM—this is needed because American clocks don't show 24-hour time; with a 24-hour clock, this indicator would not be necessary)
3. Alarm set indicator light
4. Power supply cable and plug

Top face
5. Alarm set button (hold this button down and use the hours or minutes buttons to set the alarm time)
6. Snooze button (turns off alarm and sets it to ring a short time later)

7. Clock set button (hold this button down and use the hours or minutes buttons to set the time)

8. Hours button (increases time by one hour; hold down to speed up time increase)

9. Minutes button (increases time by one minute; hold down to speed up time increase)

10. Small alarm turnoff switch

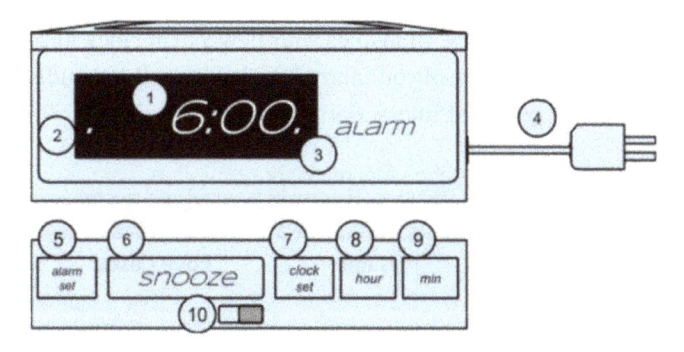

FIGURE 4-3
A standard alarm clock

Part A

Imagine that you are a person who habitually presses the snooze button, leaving you too little time to get ready, or even causing you to sleep through the alarm and miss work. At best, you tend to skip breakfast, and arrive at work groggy and unfocused.

Your challenge is to redesign the alarm clock in a way that avoids these outcomes, but still wakes you up in the calmest possible way.

Key considerations

For a user who often sleeps through the first alarm, morning is probably an anxiety-prone part of the day. Rather than solving the problem by making a louder, more jarring audio alarm, consider combining audio, visual, and/or haptic alerts in ways that make them more effective than they would be independently. Several examples from earlier in this book may prove instructive, especially the "Status Tone," "Status Shouts," and "Haptic Alerts" sections of Chapter 3. Remember also that an alarm clock is a timed trigger, and should be treated as such.

It's also worth spending a few minutes to search online for unusual approaches to alarm clocks. Clocky (*http://www.nandahome.com*), for example, is a unique alternative: equipped with wheels and a motor, it actually runs away once the alarm sounds, forcing the user to find it before it can be silenced. There are also alarm clocks that use bright light, and smartphone apps that use vibration to wake the user. Each of these has its flaws, but the general idea—that waking up doesn't have to mean getting yelled at—is worth considering.

Now fill out the following blank evaluation tool with the responses to your design exercise. And finally, what does your new alarm clock look like? Sketch out a simple picture of your alarm clock with callouts indicating key features and points of interaction.

TABLE 4-3. Calm Technology evaluation tool template

USER			
Context:	**Alert Style:**	**Usage:**	**Edge Cases:**
ENVIRONMENT			
Context:	**Alert Style:**	**Usage:**	**Edge Cases:**
INFORMATION			
Context:	**Alert Style:**	**Usage:**	**Edge Cases:**

Part B

Imagine that you sleep with a partner who works on a very different schedule from you. You wake up earlier, and they need to rest. Redesign an alarm clock that addresses this situation, making sure you wake up on time, but your partner stays asleep. And again, do it in the calmest way possible. Here are some considerations:

- How do you use lights, haptics, or tones to deal with this challenge?
- Is the alarm something that goes in your pillow, and makes a sound only you can hear?
- Is it something you wear?
- Does it take advantage of the geometry of your bedroom, with a visual alert that can only be seen from one side of the bed?

Now fill out the evaluative tool for this exercise in the same way you did for Part A. Make a sketch of this new alarm clock. What about it is different from the one you made before? What did you learn from the first exercise that you'd apply here?

EXERCISE 2: A CLOCK THAT STARTS THE DAY

This set of exercises plays off of an idea first proposed by Mark Weiser, in which he asked what would happen if an alarm clock could change its alert style based on what the person's day was going to be like.

Part A

At present, most alarm clocks wake people with a single, unalterable status shout. One of Weiser's initial ideas was to create specific tones that signaled the level of activity scheduled in your upcoming day—so, a person who wakes up with a busy agenda would hear, see, or feel something different from what they might experience on a lazy Saturday.

Your task in this exercise is to design the specific methods the alarm clock uses to signal these differences, in a way that is both clear and calm. Here are some considerations:

- How would the alarm clock go about waking the person?
- What status types would it use, and when?
- Would it use light, haptics, sound, or a combination?

- How would it treat snooze functions and other related adjustments?
- How would it handle edge cases where the person needs to wake up but isn't really busy?

Remember, a calm piece of technology is not always quiet. It matches its level of intrusion with the importance of the message, and takes up the minimum amount of user attention needed to do the job.

As in the exercise before, make sure to fill out an evaluation tool as you work and to draw a sketch of the device with labels for functionality.

Part B

Remember the principle that technology can communicate, but doesn't need to speak. Try a variation on the Weiser alarm clock that communicates information about the weather, without using a human's voice.

A popular device in sci-fi TV shows and films is to wake the main character up with a talking version of an alarm clock. It goes on and on about news, weather, and messages. In reality, this kind of alarm clock might be invasive, especially if someone prefers to wake up to music or silence.

This exercise is about communicating weather information in a calmer way. Think of how you could symbolize weather with a tone or other nonverbal indicator:

- Would the device use a tone that indicates some aspect of the weather at the moment of waking, or the forecast weather (temperature, chance of rain, etc.)?
- Could you extend or vary the tone to create the option of a longer, more detailed forecast to the user?
- Consider the example of the weather-colored light bulb in Chapter 3. How might you add a status light to the alarm clock to add detail and persistence to the weather report?
- Most people take several minutes after waking to begin comprehending messages. How does your clock deal with that? Does it repeat the same pattern? Make a status shout, then follow it with a persistent indicator? Something else?
- What edge cases might arise? What if the link to the weather service is down? What if a weather emergency is called? Will the alarm clock revert to a different state?

Fill out an evaluative tool form as you work and draw a sketch of the device with labels for functionality.

EXERCISE 3: A YEAR-LONG BATTERY

Design a product that has a year-long battery life and tells you when the battery is wearing out.

One of the core issues in the so-called Internet of Things is the tendency to make visually exciting objects with bright, full-color displays that are extremely battery-intensive. Unlike a digital watch that can be counted on to work for years, these devices have to be charged weekly, daily, or in some cases, multiple times a day.

Charging a device detracts from its calmness. Having to charge something interrupts usage and can lead to inconvenient or even dangerous situations, such as a phone that runs out of battery when you're lost, causing panic. And while there are less intrusive ways to charge devices (e.g., inductive charging by pad for a toothbrush or a phone), this is often a problem that doesn't need to be there in the first place. Replacing a full-color display with something simpler reduces its battery draw, but it also contributes to a calmer user experience. In many cases, it also reduces time to market, cuts production costs, and eliminates points of failure.

This is an exercise in minimalism. How do you design an object that uses the least amount of battery power and the lowest resolution of alert or display to get the same point across in a more elegant way than a full-resolution color display would?

Part A

Choose a single app on your smartphone, and design a standalone device that serves the same function (e.g., calendar, camera, digital notebook, stopwatch, boarding pass, digital wallet, etc.). The device must be portable, and must last approximately one year on a single battery charge, so it cannot support a color display. Here are some considerations:

- What is the bare minimum of information that needs to be displayed in order for the device to fulfill its purpose?
- How can you use simple visual alerts (LEDs, E Ink, alphanumeric displays, etc.) and/or simple audio tones to convey useful information to the user? (Haptics are too power-hungry.) It need not

give all the detail that a smartphone app does, only what it's useful to know at a short glance—a calendar, for example, could simply show which hours of the day you will be busy.

- What would be the ideal form factor for your device? Is it wearable? Does it attach to something else? Does it go in your pocket?

And finally, draw a picture of the device and fill out the evaluation tool.

Part B

Now that you've designed the device, determine how it communicates its current battery status. Remember, it's a device that lasts a year on a charge, so the indicator need only ensure that the device doesn't go dead unexpectedly, but it should do so in a way that doesn't significantly deplete battery life. Consider different lights and tones (haptics, again, are too power-hungry for this scenario).

As before, your solution should take the form of a diagram with callouts, and a completed evaluation tool.

EXERCISE 4: A CALMER KITCHEN

Because so many people use so many devices in the kitchen, competition and trial and error have made many kitchen devices reasonably functional and effective. Unfortunately, the kitchen is also a hectic, sometimes crowded space where multiple activities are being pursued simultaneously. So while most kitchen appliances do their jobs well, there's still room for improvement in making them context-appropriate.

In this exercise, your challenge is to design a calmer version of an existing piece of kitchen technology.

Pick a piece of technology in your kitchen whose alert style annoys you, and describe the device and its function. What alert style does the kitchen appliance use? How does it catch your attention, and what for? Why is it annoying to you or someone around you? If applicable, what in the environment gets in the way of the device?

How might you change the alert style or user experience of the device to improve it? Fill out an evaluation tool and draw a diagram of the modifications you'd make to the device in order to make it fit into your world better.

EXERCISE 5: A FRIDGE FOR HEALTHIER EATING

Design a refrigerator that creates a positive feedback loop that encourages healthier eating habits.

Imagine, for a moment, that someone designed a refrigerator that makes an increasingly loud, annoying tone every time you open it, in order to discourage snacking. While such a solution might be effective in the short run, it has several problems as well:

- It suffers from edge case problems—what if a diabetic friend visiting the apartment suffered a hypoglycemic episode, and had to wake up the host in order to get food? Or worse, failed to eat soon enough out of fear of disturbing them?
- It reduces human freedom and autonomy. Instead of learning what to eat and when to eat, the fridge discourages and shames the person using it, making them despise the fridge and feel bad about it, and ultimately causing them to get rid of the fridge.
- It may actually exacerbate the problem. The fridge might lead the user to simply eat out instead, preventing the fridge from monitoring their use, or maybe they would snack on premade packaged goods instead of fresh vegetables from the fridge.

So what's the underlying goal here? The goal is a refrigerator that helps people to change their behavior. Behavior change with technology works well with encouragement. It should be actionable, immediate, and come with a clear call to action. What does it mean to be immediate and actionable? Think of a time when you drove down the street past a road sign indicating your current speed. Most people will slow down immediately. Compare this to the expected outcome of watching a TV ad about driving slowly in school zones.

Consider the following:

- How do you redesign the refrigerator so that it results in positive behavior?
- What alert styles would you use?
- Would you use this fridge yourself?
- How might you design for edge cases?

EXERCISE 6: USING AMBIENT AWARENESS

This exercise is about bringing relevant, real-time data to the home or office in a less intrusive way.

We covered the concept of Natalie Jeremijenko's Live Wire, a mid-'90s art project at Xerox PARC that involved a plastic rope hanging from the ceiling, in Chapter 3. The Live Wire employed ambient awareness through the visual aspect of the wire itself and the sound the wire made as network traffic ran through it—it was connected to the company network and made a whirring noise when more bytes were moving through the system. Employees of PARC could gather around it and discuss what might be happening on the internal computer systems. Your task is to use aspects of Live Wire to design your own ambient awareness tool for your home or workplace. For instance, a stock indicator object might consist of an orb placed on the desktop that glows green when a stock is doing well and red when it is not.

Or maybe you'd like to make a product that sits in your living room and starts to glow when a bus is nearing your section of town. Keep in mind that while a sudden status change is jarring, but a pulse or soft color change can signal without disruption. With the bus example, a light in your living room could get brighter and brighter as it approaches the stop, stay stable while the bus is there, and then slowly diminish in brightness as the bus leaves.

Consider the following questions:

- What is a piece of information you find yourself looking up repeatedly? Is it the weather, a stock price or sports score, or perhaps a notification that a child got to school safely? The thickness of ice on a pond? Amount of rain in a day? When a bus is nearing your house?

- What type of information is this? Is it the sort of thing where you only need to know a general value, or, like the bus arrival time, is there a particular value you need to know about?

- How will your device indicate the information over time? Is the device standalone or something that lives on your computer? Is it visual, auditory, haptic, or wearable? The answer to this question will depend heavily upon the context in which you use it.

When you're done brainstorming and answering these questions, draw a diagram of the device with callouts for functionality and any other necessary information and pair it with an evaluation tool.

EXERCISE 7: BRINGING HAPTICS INTO PLAY

Up until now, you've been able to use any kind of status alert that you like. This exercise is focused on forcing you to take advantage of one of the calmest yet least utilized status types—the haptic alert. As you might recall from Chapter 3, a haptic alert uses the sense of touch to communicate something to a user. You can utilize touch in many different ways, and this exercise is a way to explore that.

Your task is to take an interaction in your everyday environment that currently communicates using audible or visible alerts, and modify it to use a haptic notification. Here are some considerations:

- What object, dataset, or system would you use?
- What message(s) would you be sending to the user? Why?
- How could you disable or enable the buzzing? Would there be an interface or a set of taps?
- Would you use single buzzes or a set of buzzes that vary in length, speed, or intensity to carry the message across? Could it be something besides a buzz (e.g., pressure, temperature, or texture)?
- What kinds of edge cases could arise from miscommunication of haptic alerts? How would your device help to ameliorate this?

When you're done brainstorming and answering these questions, draw a diagram of the device with callouts for functionality and any other necessary information, and pair it with an evaluation tool.

And finally, would you use this device on a daily basis? Why or why not? Ask others around you whether they like the device or not and gather their opinions. It's helpful to get more perspectives than just your own, especially for a device that makes use of less common indicators, like haptics.

Conclusions

Hopefully these exercises have helped you think about designing technology in a couple of different ways. Unless you're lucky enough to work with your own team without any client input, you'll need to work with others on design projects and understand their needs and perspectives.

The next chapter is about explaining Calm Technology in your organization. We'll discuss how to remove roadblocks and communicate with management in order to get the best products out there, and minimize both user issues and the need for ongoing support.

These are the key takeaways from this chapter:

- Use the Calm Technology evaluation tool to examine how technologies fit into their environments.

- Consider what advantages status tones, ambient awareness, and haptics can bring to your product.

- Have you found a piece of technology that bothers you, but you don't know why? Use the tools in this chapter to examine it more closely to understand how it annoys you. Use the principles of Calm Technology from Chapter 2 and the calm communication patterns from Chapter 3 to see if it could be made better.

- Don't limit your exploration of design to these exercises alone. Consider using the evaluation tool to work with other technologies in your everyday life.

[5]

Calm Technology in Your Organization

AT THIS POINT, WE'VE established the value of Calm Technology in an abstract sense, but **making the case for incorporating it into a specific project or embedding it in an organization is another task entirely.** To begin with, it's worth asking why Calm Technology is valuable as an organizational principle.

Why do you need Calm Technology in your organization? Most directly, it's a powerful organizing idea that can provide clear goals for setting limitations and reduce the risk of overdesigning the end product. This ultimately reduces costs for assembly, support, and use.

You might think you're saving money by getting to market as quickly as possible, without spending a ton of effort calming down your user experience, but **think of the longer-term outcome.** A less calm, fussier interface means more confused users, more calls to tech support, and more need for patches and updates down the line. Design for calmness now and you'll save money later, when it really counts.

Building Teams for Calm Technology

Calm Tech is best worked on using **lean principles**, which means, more than anything, reducing the number of stakeholders involved in a project. **Teams with fewer stakeholders get things done faster, are more likely to take risks**, and have the ability to make mistakes without fear of career failure or retribution from colleagues or higher-ups.

You can reduce stakeholder numbers in several ways. One tactic that's proven surprisingly effective is to set **low expectations** for the project, which tends to discourage executives from getting involved. As the project comes to a close, you can then invite stakeholders to join in, allowing them to share in the credit without feeling the need to provide input just for input's sake.

Key stakeholders, on the other hand, should be sold on the principle of Calm Technology as much as possible, allowing the team something to fall back on when the inevitable request for additional features arises. Find someone on the client side or in your organization who has a knack for advocating, and task them with winning over individuals who could potentially shut you down. Managers who are in a position to become jealous of the project should be involved as much as possible early on, as a way of preventing them from hijacking it further down the line.

It's crucial to remember that, no matter how promising the program, it only takes one person at the managerial level to start or stop it. This isn't usually a sign of malice or incompetence, either—most often, it's because they want to **build something** and **feel important**, too.

THE RULE OF FIVE

Why five? **Teams larger than five are prone to run into communication difficulties and operational constraints.** There's an overhead associated with conducting communication among multiple members, and each additional person on a team increases it. Ultimately, too many people on a team fosters a slow, meeting-oriented culture with **less autonomy.** Until you scale the team up, a team of fewer than five can do a lot. In many cases, even two competent, self-directed people are plenty to get a project started.

What if you have a project so large that it needs more than five people just to get the work done? **Split the team up** into smaller working groups and be forthcoming on what each one of them needs to do on the project. Make sure there are people who **love to communicate** on each team, and have them blog or write internally about what each team is doing, so that everyone stays in the loop.

What if you can't get a team down to five because of "internal stakeholders"? Sometimes you might get into a difficult spot where managers and stakeholders get involved in your project. Often this takes the form of a boss telling you that "we know you want to have a lean team focused on this feature set, but we need you to have these people involved in the process."

This is a tough issue. **With many stakeholders needing buyoff on a project, it may be difficult to get anything done.** It's difficult to get the people you need on your team to do work without the expectations of fitting into the existing structure. One way to help is to **beta test your people.**

TEST YOUR TEAM

Think of your project team like a band. Bands need to practice before their first big show, and so do you.

Do a small test project first to see how the team works together. Even an hour-long exercise of designing a new toy or a product for fun will expose your team to the experience of creating something within a time limit, and will give you some inkling of what conflicts might exist among them. It also helps the team learn how to work with one another, and gives you the chance to address friction points before they turn into inescapable political roadblocks. You can then work on any conflicts and reduce them together, or minimize interaction between incendiary people on a team.

Start by asking your team members what they're interested in doing and how they might contribute to the project, and *then* launch into the test project. Sometimes anxiety is produced by projects that are too big where there's too much at stake, and sometimes people want to be part of project teams without actually putting in the work, for reasons of political safety. Employees can be concerned for their reputation if the product fails, so they might be hesitant to work on a product in any other way than what they're used to, or to implement new features that are foreign to them. In these cases, **it is important to carve out a sense of creative safety** on the team. Create a place where people can explore ideas that differ from those they're used to, without fear of managerial reprisal.

HIRE DIFFERENTLY FROM YOU

A team should have **diverse perspectives**, or else you're missing an opportunity to spot better solutions. You want to make a team that respects the differences and allows for everyone to be at their best.

You need people. You also need people who will call your bluff when you try to make something that's only usable by those who make a six-figure salary. You need people who live in messier or cleaner environments than you, and people from countries and ethnic backgrounds different from yours.

Additionally, you might find someone at your company who understands the industry but does not know how to speak the language of stakeholders. Find someone else to translate it for the stakeholders, or be the translator yourself.

Regardless of who they are and where they come from, **take what your team members have to say very seriously, especially if they're passionate about it**. If upper-level management can't handle honest feedback, then work as a translator so material is presented in a way that is more "managerial and safe." Setting low expectations for the product, as discussed earlier, makes this job easier—translation's not so hard when the reputations of managers aren't on the line.

FIND POLITICAL BUFFERS

Organizational politics are often tedious and get in the way of teams doing their best work, but they're a reality in even the most effective organizations. **Find a supporter for your project who can act as a political buffer so you can get your work done**. Either add them to your team so that they share the load, or meet with them frequently. This small investment of effort and time will free up you and your team to actually get things done. If you're in a traditional organization, consider having someone write weekly reports to managers.

Often you might be tempted to write reports that contain only positive outcomes, but in reality, managers need to know the negative as well. If you don't tell management anything, their minds will likely wander into a negative and paranoid zone that can be far worse than the reality you're trying to sugarcoat. Instead, show slow, measured growth over time—they'll sleep easier knowing you're on your way to achieving your goals. And that weekly report is ammo for them to bring to the board, to keep the project going if it comes to that.

Weekly update reports are also a good way to ask managers for help. It's all about making it easier for your managers to work. If you tell them what is bad, it's not a surprise. Make sure they find out before their supervisors do.

Design for Privacy

Privacy is one of the most important considerations today and will become increasingly important in the future. As we transition from the industrial society to the information society, we'll see more and more examples where people's real lives are affected by privacy and security breaches. As I'm writing this book, the Ashley Madison hack is still front-page news, raising the specter of privacy violations seriously impacting people's lives on a grand scale.

Practice privacy by design versus privacy by disaster. **Privacy considerations should be incorporated into every aspect of an app's lifecycle**, as well as your product's web presence, legal agreements, user experience, messaging, and development.

It's no longer about whether your site or product will be attacked or not. It's a matter of when. **Large or small, your product or service *will* be messed with at some point in time.** Get used to it! This is the future, and the future comes with bugs, viruses, and hacking attacks. Act now or be forced to act later. Don't be afraid, be prepared! The consequences will be greater if you aren't. Be careful out there. It's going to get even hairier as more and more devices become a part of our lives. Keep abreast of the current industry and its regulations. **Fight for your users and they will fight for you.**

The following guidelines can help you to design a product with privacy and security in mind.

THE USER EXPERIENCE OF PRIVACY

Great privacy user experience means that your users will understand the privacy policy you created when they start to use your app. A well-built app will let users know what they're opting into when they use your software.

Though your app or product might require access to a person's photos, locations, and contacts, they'll likely not want to share this information every time they interact with the product. Allow them to turn sharing on or off at the point of interaction or content creation.

Present privacy controls at the point of content creation. Display these controls for every piece of content that can be created or shared in a given system. Instagram does this reasonably well, as users can choose whether to place a photo on a map when they create a piece of content. You should follow these guidelines:

- Empower your users.
- Offer on/off switches and simple settings.
- Make it easy to access controls such as alert styles or tones and volume levels.
- Don't hide it all behind complex menus; create physical buttons when possible.

GET A PRIVACY POLICY

Think about it. Running an Internet-connected product or service isn't the same as just providing a physical product to someone. You're taking and caring for a piece of them at the same time. **You're not just hosting their data—you're hosting *them*!** It's a big responsibility. Hosting user data is a privilege, not a right. Privacy policies are regret-management tools. Legislation being put in place will increasingly require these.

People need to be able to read your policy and understand what they can expect by using your product in under a minute. The best way to do this is to **separate your privacy policy into two sections:** *plain English* **and** *legalese*. Write the policy in English first, then get your lawyer to write it up more formally, as well as helping with the plain-text version. Post both on your site or include them with your product.

The most basic privacy policy should at the very least answer the following questions:

- What data does your product or service collect, and why your product or service need to collect that data?
- What will this user data be used for? Why should your users share it?

- Where can your users go to **permanently delete** their accounts and ensure their data is removed from your servers?

- Where can users go to **download the data** that's been gathered by your product? Users need to be able to migrate if your service closes. It is your privilege to temporarily host user data. **It's their data, not yours.** And as a provider of a product, you are in your user's debt. Your users allow your company or product to exist, and they should be respected. **Respect them, and they'll respect you.**

- What precautions have you taken to ensure your users' **personal lives** will not be affected if your company is hacked?

- How do you notify users of updates to your privacy policy? Consider creating a practice of notifying users of any changes to the privacy policy at least 30 days before the new policies are put into place. Show **abbreviated changes** to the privacy policy and track them so that users can see the differences in the policies.

- What are you doing to ensure transparency? **Use transparency to build trust by telling people what their data will be used for.**

This outline is a good start. And it will also bring up questions to your engineering team on how data is stored and protected to begin with.

ANTICIPATE AND EXPECT SECURITY BREACHES

Security breaches are organic manifestations, not mechanical ones. They come from two places: people looking for ways to take advantage of or get data and personal information out, or people simply playing with systems to see if they can work around them or break them. A lot of this is done unofficially, not by people with nine-to-five hours, but by people playing in their free time. **The best thing to do is to get to know and respect these people. And hire them!** Security is a difficult thing to get support for, even with all of the hacks that are currently going on, because investing the money doesn't net returns. Most companies don't allocate resources for attacks until they've happened. Then they spend a lot of money fixing hacked systems, when the hacks could have been prevented if security principles had been adopted in the early stages of product development.

Selling Calm Technology to Managers

The typical management response to Calm Technology, or any way of doing things that's different from the norm, is skepticism. That's fine—they're just doing their jobs. It's your job to get them past their skepticism and into a place of advocacy.

Most of this task lies in **anticipating objections, and responding in a calm, reasoned, and sympathetic way.** I've included a few of the most common objections here, and ways you might respond to them.

OBJECTION 1: MORE FEATURES ARE BETTER

Why do some executives push for so many features to begin with? Often they see successful products that have been around for a long time, and have already proven themselves in the market.

What they're seeing is a mature product. What they don't see is the lower-featured, often-messy product that the company originally released, before it got big. Things always start small and grow; what we see later is the finished product. There's nothing wrong with starting with the end in mind, but it's important to recognize the steps along the way. In the same way that you don't see all of the revisions of a painting at a gallery, you don't see the revisions a successful product has gone through when you purchase it or read about it in the press.

Solution

In this case, **management needs to be educated about the history of successful products and how they really grow**: sustainable development, one or two main features per season, and an interaction with their community.

The best approach, then, is often to develop a presentation that gives examples of products with few features that make a lot of money. It may sound very simple, but this is often exactly the "insurance" managers need in order to sign off. The key to getting it right is providing a sense of understanding and comfort: that other companies have done a good job of this, that what you're doing is not unknown or wild, and that there is a planned path for success. Sometimes this means incorporating a feature schedule into the project so that you space out feature releases well into the future. This is often a good strategy for staving off adding features until there's time to incorporate them thoughtfully.

How can this go wrong? The executive might have already sold all of the features through the sales team, and now you need to incorporate all of them. In this case, you don't have a lot of leeway, and may have no choice but to make the product that's already being paid for. But if you have any hand in initiating the design and user experience of the product, and can show a feasible roadmap, then showing fewer features and getting executives comfortable is a good approach.

OBJECTION 2: ALL OF THE LEGACY FEATURES MUST STAY

Have you ever had an executive on a project who has "pet features" or encountered a product with legacy features that "absolutely must stay in"? This can be a difficult situation. Legacy features have a bad habit of preventing newer (and often superior) approaches from being implemented. More often, they make for a cluttered user interface or product usage flow. On the other hand, there are a few tricks available for making legacy features easier to deal with.

Solution

Often what you really need to do is show someone the product is wrong without forcing them to take responsibility for the decision—some outside, objective force needs to do the telling. The first thing to **determine is whether the market is actually using all those elegant features**; product trials, user testing, and statistical analysis can help here. You may discover that some features are useful and others are not, and you'll have the data to back up your opinions. Some features might be used by a small number of people but be crucial to them. In this case, it may be possible to demote the legacy features in the user interface if they're not as important for everyday use.

Another way to solve this problem is to **create a "light" version of the product** to help users get into it without overwhelming them. Adobe used this idea to great effect, releasing a cheaper version of its full Photoshop product called Photoshop Elements. It worked well enough to introduce people to the basic concepts of photo editing and some of Photoshop's tools without overwhelming them. This allowed for a new generation and section of the market to pick up Photoshop and integrate it into their workflow, more than doubling Adobe's addressable market in just a few years.

At the last company I worked at, a single stakeholder had complete control over one page of the website. He loaded it with as many features as he could. Then we launched the site with our design and included his single feature-laden page in the launch. We ran statistics to see if anyone was using the page, and when we found that no one was visiting it, we were able to present a data-backed argument to remove the page (and eventually to release a pared-down, redesigned version in line with the rest of the site).

OBJECTION 3: WHAT ABOUT ALL THE OTHER STAKEHOLDERS?

Big projects almost always bring significant expectations, and often back themselves into the corner of not being able to fail. Such projects can also be significantly overfunded, which—counterintuitively—can often lead to poor resource allocation. Risks are not taken if the project is too high profile, for fear of job loss. Sometimes people are so wrapped up in a project that they forget about the outside work, especially in very large, political organizations. In short, **the more stakeholders you have internally, the more you are building a product for your managers, not the users outside of the company.**

Many managers may have input on a product, each with something at stake. Therefore, they must be involved.

Solution

Encourage the team members to help you with research, or bring them into the field while you test the products.

OBJECTION 4: THERE'S NO TIME FOR USER TESTING

There's no time for user research, or testing can only be done in-house with a lab of people paid to come in and use the product under sterile conditions, because the product must be kept absolutely secret.

Solution

Set up an in-house environment that replicates the use of the product in the real world as much as possible (e.g., a checkout lane, living room, office, school, playground, parking lot, museum, etc.), and use your own team members as testers. You can use cardboard and paper prototypes to reduce costs.

OBJECTION 5: THE PRODUCT MUST STAY SECRET UNTIL LAUNCH

"You can't show this to anyone, even outside testers, until we know we got it! You could get fired if you show this to anyone outside of the company!"

More often than not, **extremely secret projects result in products that flop.** What we now know as the Microsoft PixelSense was originally introduced in 2007 as a massive, table-sized tablet with a 30-inch rear projection display. Dubbed the Microsoft Surface, the product was kept under tight controls. It had a hefty price tag (over $10,000) and was inaccessible to developers. When the 9.7-inch Apple iPad was released in 2010, I joked that it was a "miniature" Microsoft Surface. The form factor was smaller, it was cheaper, and it had a multi-touch screen. I lamented that Microsoft had kept the Surface so close to its vest. It made it more difficult for the product to catch on in the market. In October 2012, Microsoft released its own smaller tablet device, retaining the Surface name. The larger Microsoft Surface was renamed the PixelSense, and served by Samsung SUR40 with Microsoft PixelSense, and the name Surface was reserved for the smaller tablet. Though Microsoft reported $853 million in revenue from Surface sales during the 2013 fiscal year, it spent over $900 million on marketing and advertising for a product that consumers didn't respond well to. In addition, Microsoft had recently risked redesigning its core operating system, capped by the release of the ill-fated and difficult to use Windows 8. Microsoft learned its lesson, though, and didn't give up—the Surface 2 and Surface 3 did much better, and so did future releases of Microsoft Windows. By January 2015, sales of the Surface had reached $1 billion. The Windows 10 operating system debuted in July 2015 and was a stable release perfectly suited for mobile tablets. The future of Microsoft Surface and its other new products such as the Microsoft Surface Book (a laptop offering) and the Surface Hub (an interactive smartboard) are yet to be seen, but Microsoft slowly improved on its products.

Solution

This is one of the most difficult arguments to battle. Many companies, in fact, have intellectual property (IP) issues and a legitimate concern about product leaks, so showing the product to the outside world might not be allowed by corporate policy. On the other hand, the longer a product is developed without external feedback, the more likely it is to fall into an **echo chamber** of features and interfaces that make sense to the developers, but not the users.

So, rather than fighting a losing battle to show it to the world, work instead to get feedback internally. **An organization that's large enough to have IP concerns is large enough to have coworkers who are completely unfamiliar with the project.**

Internal usage is a good litmus test for the outside world. If a product is good enough that it spreads internally, and people *voluntarily* use the product at the company, then the product may well succeed outside of the company. That is how Gmail spread, in fact: first internally at Google and then as an externally released product.

Entering a Product into Human Society: A Calm Product Launch

Technology might be ready for humans, but humans are not always ready for tech.

Shortsightedness and a misunderstanding of how long it takes to get something to market, or how long it takes to get users to understand a new concept, often get in the way of organizations actually getting a real product to market. When elevators were first introduced in modern skyscrapers, for example, they had to be artificially slowed down so that humans could handle them.

How can you make sure that the product you're building is a fit for the people who are going to use it? We can tackle this question by examining successful product launches. **Very rarely does a product initially hit the market in its final, successful form.** Instead, it evolves with users over time to eventually fit into their lives. By doing user research and understanding what the market needs, you can save yourself the disappointment (not to mention cost) of a failed product launch.

You might have a great product, but the way you introduce it to the world matters just as much. Release it too soon or don't explain the product well enough, and people may be confused by it, or worse, fear it. You might have a product that sits on supermarket shelves and is never purchased. Or you might release too many features at the same time without understanding who your market is or how people will use the technology.

Launch processes are important because they rely on an understanding of social norms. When we said in Chapter 3 that technology should respect social norms, we were talking about the launch process as well. Showing the device used in its intended environment is good, but it's even more important to **allow people to play with it**, and come up with their own solutions and uses for it.

How does a product launch work? It's important to determine where it will be launched, to whom you will launch, how much of the product will be tested, and how you'll price it. It's important to have a small group of people test the product in the real world, and not to be especially secretive about it. **If fans spread the information for you, it's priceless**.

REFINE

If good design reduces the number of steps to get to the goal, **Calm Design reduces the amount of attention to get to the goal**. For every feature or system you add to the product, ask yourself, "Is this really necessary? Is there a better or cheaper way we could do it? Something less resource intensive with fewer moving parts or lines of code?" It often works to assign steep constraints when designing something. Limitations lead to cleverness and a lot of thought around what can and cannot be done. Often teams with too much time and too many resources overdesign a product, whereas some that are forced to build with limited resources end up doing very well.

You must also have a lot of passion around the product. Apple cofounder Steve Wozniak wanted his own personal computer badly, but didn't have the money for it. He thought about computer design all of the time. What if he could make a working computer from cheap components? The more he thought about it, the more he developed a model of the computer in his head, and then he began removing components until it became very cheap. The result eventually became the Apple I and II, revolutionizing the home computer industry and igniting a whole new generation of software developers.

The products that do things the most efficiently will win in the future. Reduce the steps required to get to a goal. Find out what people are trying to do with your product or service, and map out the interaction.

Don't settle when you reach the really hard work. The more you put into the design process, the less you'll have to support the system in the future—and the less money you'll have to spend on it over time.

COMPETITION

I've often encountered companies that postpone launches until the product is "perfect" for fear of competition and copycats. This often harms the company and the launch.

Consider the social network space. Friendster, Tribe, and MySpace all preceded Facebook, and numerous other social networks have tried to challenge its success. But Facebook is the dominant social network, not because it was the first to market or because it copycatted someone else, but because it rapidly implemented new features and grew with its users over time. **It was the best implementation because it didn't stop implementing.** This gave it the best user experience.

Fears of predatory competition in the tech sphere are often overblown. Stagnation is where you should direct your fear. The distinct advantage that a startup has over a larger company isn't necessarily that its ideas are better, but that it can act more quickly. A larger company might spend six months deliberating over a launch process, whereas a startup might try something for two days, figure out whether it worked or failed, and try another entirely different process by the end of the week. **Decision paralysis has killed more companies than knockoffs.**

Letting a product gain fans organically means it is more real than a glossy marketing campaign. Use real pictures of people using the product and let them tell their own stories. You may have personas you're developing for, but how the product is actually used and by whom may surprise you. And finally, honor your customers and remember that you're making products to serve them. Routinely check in with your support team to see what the top problems are, and learn from them how you might be able to solve them with a better interface or product design in the next release.

DO THE RESEARCH!

William Gibson famously wrote **"the future is unevenly distributed."** The best way to ensure your product doesn't fall prey to the mistakes people have made in the past is to study it.

I've spent the majority of my career doing some kind of user experience work. I later built a startup that made products used by millions. A lot of my life has been spent predicting whether products will work or not and advising companies on those products, and getting paid to do **user experience analysis means thinking deeply about the entire experience of a product.**

I often see entire systems and industries going back in time because they don't learn from the past, they try to enter too many new products and features into the market at once, or they make false assumptions about design. These are very costly mistakes. Google Glass is an extreme example, but there are thousands.

Research is not a "luxury"—it is a crucial part of the design process. In addition to saving money and time, **good research gives certainty to what is "real" versus what is assumed.** Once you begin looking at and understanding how to do the research around the product you'd like to build, you might find that much of the research has already been done.

Many academic institutions have created products and services before, and startups too. Then they write about them. Using academic archives and the Internet Archive (*https://www.archive.org*) is very helpful, as is asking established people in the industry whether they've seen or built products like yours in college or at companies.

It may seem counterintuitive when you're trying to make technology that works in the future, but going back in time is very helpful. Yes, some research papers may not be so readable, but you'll be able to get the gist quickly once you get used to it. Some are from capstone projects, others are from people who spent four or five years working toward a degree and then left for a full-time job or to work on something else. Many of these research papers were written for educational purposes, so students could get a handle on concepts before turning professional. Consider Georgia Tech, Carnegie Mellon, NYU, Stanford, the MIT Media Lab, and RISD. Also look at PARC research and try to contact those who generated the original ideas or made the mistakes. Sometimes you may be able to work with them!

ALLOW TIME FOR REAL-WORLD TESTING

It is crucial for executives and managers to allow enough time after a product has been built for real-world testing, small beta test groups, and code reliability testing. Often executives sell customers on features, not functionality, and the features don't have enough time to be tested before they go to market.

A company can easily get caught up in building a product, but forget to sanity check with the outside world. One of the ways to ensure that a product will be successful when it is launched is to do a small product launch before going into larger production.

It is best to test products while you're making them, instead of doing all of the testing at the very end. Doing so can save lots of time and money, because you may be able to catch design mistakes early on. If you can't get the go-ahead to test your product, put someone in a room with it and tell them to figure out how to use it. What they don't immediately figure out can be designed better or shown to them on the front of the box.

DON'T REDESIGN THE ENTIRE THING AT ONCE

Do you have a system in place that's already useful that people are already trained on? Many companies fall prey to the "let's redesign everything!" catch. This can come from executives and developers in equal parts. Perhaps developers are sick of the time it takes to maintain and test code, and stakeholders want to add new features or cut costs. But be forewarned. A complete redesign can be one of the riskiest things a company can do. Redesigning an entire system or piece of software means that the old product still has to be supported, and the new product will have bugs and have to be supported at the same time. Edge cases will double, and it could take years before the system is stable again.

It's often better to improve a system slowly over time than to redesign it and replace it with a more complex, newer system. Having people stop to learn new systems can lead to mistakes, but learning a new workflow one piece at a time gives people a chance to get comfortable with changes.

Call your customer service department and figure out what the most frequent issue is. Tech support probably encounters the same issues from people again and again. **What are the most common complaints? Solve those first, and make your way down to the bottom, bit by bit.** It's often the hardest stuff to fix that makes the biggest impact, but fixing simple items can sometimes improve the product greatly. You're not trying to replace tech support; you're just helping them do a better job with the calls that come in. Work with your designers and developers to address and fix the first issue. Then tackle the next issues in support.

If you get enough of these issues and are skilled and experienced enough to do a complete redesign, then go through with it, but be aware that some major sites (such as Digg and StumbleUpon) have completely lost user traction after overarching redesigns.

DESIGN FOR HUMAN-HUMAN INTERACTION

Temptation is strong to use tech to replace people, rather than **improve and streamline the interaction** *between* **people**—and yet this is often tech's most useful role. How many times has the muscle memory of your own fingers taken you to Google? What does Google do but connect human knowledge to other humans? What does Facebook do but connect people to one another in a faster way? Slack allows people to connect to one another with less friction and overhead than email. In these systems, the technology dissolves and becomes invisible.

The most powerful human technology brings people together. Early examples might be the written word, ritual, or song. Each of these systems was designed to connect people. When you're really into a book, you don't notice the pages anymore. You imagine what the writer is trying to tell you. You're connected to the mind of the writer. That's what the best technology does. The interface of the tech disappears and you interface with another person, community, or idea. Early bulletin board software didn't have images, but it brought people together.

DESIGN FOR OPTIMUM BATTERY LIFE

Battery life will improve over time, but the best way to preserve it is to **design simple, efficient systems**. You don't want to leave someone stranded when a battery wears out.

For instance, I use a digital key code door locking system at my house. I quickly learned to rely on the digital system. It's so convenient that I stopped bringing my key. I don't have to worry about being locked out of my house when the batteries on the door lock run out—which happens about once a year—because the keypad **flashes red** when it's **nearing battery depletion**, giving me plenty of time to change the batteries.

Conclusions

Hopefully this chapter has helped you to understand more deeply the concept of a calm product launch and some of the strategies you can employ to ensure a product is adequately tested before giving it to the public. There is no right or wrong path for product design and development as long as you consider who is going to use it, the ways in which it could go wrong, and the areas of people's lives you're going to affect. Paying close attention to user needs and rapidly iterating with respect to your users will always serve you well. The products that respect users the most win.

Some things to keep in mind:

- **Team size matters.** Teams with fewer stakeholders get things done quickly, and are more likely to take risks. Each additional person on a team increases communication barriers.

- **Discover your team's strengths and weakness and see how they work together through a test project.** Just an hour-long exercise of designing a new toy or a product for fun will expose your team to the experience of creating something within a time limit, and will give you some inkling of what conflicts might exist among them.

- **Perspective matters. Find people who work differently from you.** A team should be made up of different kinds of people from different backgrounds, or you may miss edge cases. Not all users are alike, and your team shouldn't be either.

- **Internal support is important.** If you work for a bureaucratic or political company, make sure to get support from internally trusted people for your project. Find a way to explain it in the language understood by the company. Translate your vision into theirs.

- **Constrain requirements.** For every feature or system you add to the product, ask yourself, "Is this really necessary? Is there a better or cheaper way we could do it?"

- **Do your homework.** Most projects that have failed before failed for a reason.

- **Respect user privacy. Your product is a service to them, not you.**

[6]

The History and Future of Calm Technology

XEROX PARC (PALO ALTO Research Center) was founded in 1970 as the Research & Development Lab of the Xerox Corporation. The name "Xerox" today is most commonly associated with copiers and printers, but from the '70s to the late '90s, Xerox PARC was a hub of alternative and groundbreaking computing research, spanning every type of technological device imaginable. The number of breakthrough innovations that emerged from PARC in the '70s is legendary, from precursors to the modern graphic user interface, object-oriented programming, and desktop publishing to the first widespread adoption of Douglas Engelbart's mouse.

FIGURE 6-1
PARC researchers in 1972, two years after founding. PARC's office spaces were filled with people from different disciplines, allowing for different thinking about computing in general.[*]

---

[*] Image courtesy of PARC Research; used with permission.

My focus in this book has been on a somewhat later chapter in PARC's history: a body of work whose real value is just now starting to reveal itself. In the 1980s, three PARC researchers—Mark Weiser, John Seely Brown, and Rich Gold—began to envision a future in which people interacted with many small devices in their lives, what Weiser called "pads, tabs, and boards." Their work took place long before mobile devices had any real computing power, yet they managed to make working prototypes of a mobile phone, a digital tablet, and an interactive work board, and write extensively about the experience of and best practices for using them. It was, in a very small and controlled way, a living, breathing example of life with Ubiquitous Computing.

Videoconferencing Before Skype

Among the hundreds—maybe thousands—of innovations that researchers at Xerox PARC were playing with years before they became widely available, videoconferencing is one of the most noteworthy. In the late 1980s PARC engineers began installing dedicated video and audio links between different parts of the campus, and soon thereafter they had the ability to videoconference with remote research teams in other cities. But what's really striking about these systems, besides just how early on they were being used, was the sense of effortless ease and calm they seemed to instill in the researchers who used them.

For most of us, a modern-day chat via Skype, FaceTime, or Google Hangouts is sort of a necessary evil, and a major source of anxiety. Choppy pictures, hung connections, unsynchronized audio, and confusing interfaces are still common occurrences, and while the benefits of video communication generally outweigh these problems, few of us would call video chat an "encalming" experience.

By all accounts, though, videoconferencing at PARC *was* encalming, because it worked so well. It didn't hang up. There was plenty of bandwidth. Everyone knew how to use it. It was optimized for a small set of tasks, and it did them very well. In part, this was a natural outcome of working in an environment where there were only a few hundred users, and all of them are technophiles. But it was also a result of limitations. Because everything at PARC was built from scratch, often at great expense, there was rarely more technology present than was absolutely necessary. There was very little legacy to adhere to, and building new tools or applications from scratch was the norm. Resource availability was a given. Building fault tolerance into technology was a low priority, because the creators of the technology also had some degree of control over the system it relied upon.

Technology at PARC, therefore, was lean and highly focused—the exact opposite of our modern multiparadigm, commercially driven world. Their world was advanced, but dramatically different from ours today. Instead of a single group of people working on technology all under one roof as they had at PARC, we have many different companies at different stages of development working on technologies in different programming languages all over the world. Many rely on conflicting paradigms and follow incompatible guidelines and rule sets. Some technologies are not managed by the engineers themselves, but are guided by those who have hired them and are responsible for making money with the products. Features are often prioritized over usability, and research from the past is not taken into account. Often, technology is entered into the world without an understanding of how it will fit into everyday life.

The Beginnings of Calm Technology

Researchers at PARC looked at "redefining the entire relationship of humans, work, and technology for the post-PC era," and their thoughts and experiments were among the first to grasp the implications of what Weiser was starting to call "Ubiquitous Computing." Although it is common today to talk about bringing "humanness" to digital interaction, at the time, the concept of humanizing technology was right at the cutting edge. The 1980s were a time when using a computer meant sitting in a code-locked room running serious programs like VisiCalc (Figure 6-2), the very first user-friendly spreadsheet software for the personal computer. Computers were business, and the challenges of computing were very functional: throughput, processing power, maximizing efficiencies. So, the idea of computing being "calm," and fitting into everyday life in a way that felt natural, or even enjoyable, was far from most people's minds.

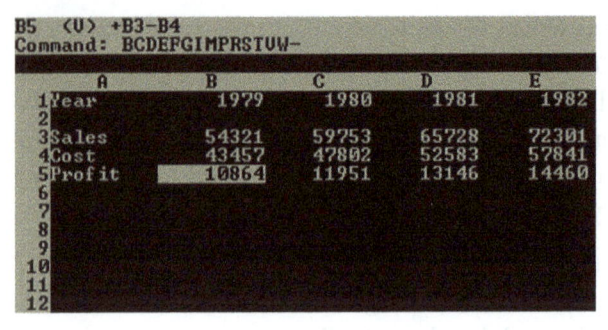

FIGURE 6-2
Screenshot of VisiCalc running on an Apple II computer.[†]

While the rest of the industry focused on the present, PARC was a place where researchers were encouraged to predict the problems of the future and solve them before they even arose. In the wake of so many advances designed to improve the capabilities of machines, Weiser and Brown chose to take on the problem of humanizing technology—specifically, **how could technology *amplify humanness* instead of taking it away?** How could great interfaces augment human intellect, not just by offering more power, but by *maximizing* what the human mind could absorb and react to?

To get some sense of what Weiser and Brown were up to, it helps to understand the context in which they were working. The environment at PARC in those days was both rigorous and wildly experimental. PARC's offices were filled with bikes, beards, and multidisciplinary nerds lounging on beanbags, passionately discussing the future of technology—not from a fearful perspective, but a deeply optimistic, humanistic one.

Those beanbag chairs offer a good example of what made PARC an ideal place for humanizing technology. More than just a comfy place to lounge while pondering the future, PARC's beanbags were a calm but powerful tool for improving communication. As the story goes, before they were introduced the engineers who worked there would often interrupt each other while writing out concepts on the blackboards, resulting in arguments, ideas left only partly expressed, and a general air of disruption. Alan Kay, a leading mind at PARC in those days,

---

[†] Image courtesy of Dan Bricklin.

had the idea of replacing the chairs in a conference room with beanbags, and worked with Lab Director Bob Taylor to make it a reality. The result was a space in which individual thoughts were given more time to make themselves known: by making it slightly more difficult for any one person to get up and go to the board, the beanbags gently directed the engineers to wait and reflect, rather than immediately interrupting as soon as an objection occurred.

Beanbag chairs in such a situation can be considered a Calm Technology because they induce an organizational tempo shift. Sitting in a beanbag rather than a regular chair changes the tempo of one's actions. You can't help but move slower.

Technology writer Venkatesh Rao suggests that shifting tempo (*http://bit.ly/tempo-rao*) within an organization allows one to do different things at different times (client presentation mode, get things done mode, launch mode, etc.). These varying tempos allow people to communicate across groups, and to think and do their work more effectively, by matching the pace with the demands of the task. Putting beanbag chairs in front of the chalkboards at PARC **slowed down the tempo of the workers, allowing for a different type of thought work.** Researchers were better able to get into a flow state with their thoughts and ideas, and their colleagues were forced to reflect more before asking a question or jumping up to collaborate.

PARC was the sort of place where passion projects were given wide scope, with the understanding that great breakthroughs often came from something as simple as a desire to do something really, really cool. Weiser himself was part of a band called Severe Tire Damage, formed with several other technologists from around Silicon Valley, who worked together to become the first livestreamed band in history[‡] (they also "opened" for the Rolling Stones, exactly once, in 1994). The streaming system Weiser and his colleagues used, called the Multicast Backbone, went on to spawn a revolution in digital media culminating in world-spanning services like Spotify and Pandora.

[‡] "Rolling Stones Live on Internet: Both a Big Deal and a Little Deal." (*http://www.nytimes.com/1994/11/22/arts/rolling-stones-live-on-internet-both-a-big-deal-and-a-little-deal.html*)

These may all sound like small details or inconsequential anecdotes, but they also tell a lot about how different Weiser and Brown were from their contemporaries outside of PARC, and how it's possible that they could have, in the mid-1980s, come up with a series of insights about human–technology interaction that are applicable today. A lot of what they did looks playful, and it was. PARC was a liminal space full of great people that provided a safe environment for new ideas, explicitly designed to counter the approach used by the standard companies of the day.

Together, Weiser and Brown oversaw several research projects at PARC over the course of their years there, and gained a reputation for granting their teams exceptional freedom to explore both software and hardware capabilities. They were, in many ways, great enablers, creating spaces for play and encouraging researchers to make things that didn't—or couldn't—exist anywhere else. Their goal, and the goal of their teams, was to create the future before it happened, and then consider its consequences for the larger world.

Mark Weiser took on the role of lab leader at Xerox PARC in 1987. John Seely Brown joined the organization two years after that, in 1990, as director of the research center. They had a fair bit in common—both had earned degrees in computer and communication science from the University of Michigan, and both had a powerful interest in the way computing systems changed over time, and how that change could be managed.

On October 5, 1996, after many years of invention and investigation, Weiser and Brown published a summary of their thoughts on the future of computing called "The Coming Age of Calm Technology." Its remarkably prescient take on the role of technology in our lives is best summed up in this early passage (emphasis added):

> The important waves of technological change are those that fundamentally alter the place of technology in our lives. *What matters is not technology itself, but its relationship to us.*

When interactions are calm, they argued, you're not getting bombarded all of the time; you're getting reassured. Great interaction design allows people to accomplish their goals at the lowest mental cost:

> There is no less technology involved in a comfortable pair of shoes, in a fine writing pen, or in delivering the New York Times on a Sunday morning, than in a home PC. Why is one often enraging, the others frequently encalming? We believe the difference is in how they engage our attention.

Weiser and Brown's paper, unfortunately, didn't do anything like enumerate a series of principles to follow—it's not a cookbook for creating Calm Technology. They did, however, write down a series of signs of Calm Technology. What would it be like if tech were calm? The two things they said were about the periphery:

- Calm Tech empowers the periphery.
- Through empowering the periphery, it allows us to attune to more than one thing without taking focus away from our primary task or our ability to be human.

This book attempts to step in where Weiser and Brown left off, to provide a detailed guide to creating Calm Technology.

We already live in an era of connected devices; we just don't think about them that way. We don't often read articles on washing machines or go to conferences on them. But these devices are there. They're powered by the first ubiquitous technology—electricity. This technology has been made invisible in our environment, so we see only the effects it has in enabling other technology to function. What would the world be like if our computers and other devices were as invisible and maintenance-free as electricity is now? Technology as Weiser and Brown imagined it would bring us back into life instead of out of it, give us joy instead of anxiety, foster community, make us more human. They envisaged a future in which we use technology as a tool and aren't used by it—where we use technology to create more than to consume, and where technology moves out of the way and reconnects us with the most important things in life: bringing us back to ourselves and our connection to other humans.

We limit ourselves if we think of technology as being something separate from us. It is the most human thing we have ever created. It is an ecosystem we are intertwined with that evolved as we evolved. Humans and technology coproduce one another, and we can learn from each other. What Guy Hoffman did with his robots was to imbue them with smoother interactions. He didn't create technology that tried to overpower us and make decisions for us. He made technology that could play in an orchestra alongside him, and improvise with him, looking back and forth between him and the instruments. Hoffman mentioned that we felt more love for appliances in the first 30 seconds of a Pixar film with a lamp in the title credit than we ever had for any appliances in our homes. And it was because of the way the appliances "acted."

Calm Technology has a long way to go, but it's time to start building environments and systems that work with us. Conserve what is good, and improve the rest. Individuals and small teams can go a long way when they're motivated to make change, so **create the change in technology you'd like to see in the world.** Be patient and it will pay off.

> *Ubiquitous computing just might help to free our minds from unnecessary work, and connect us to the fundamental challenge that humans have always had: to understand the patterns in the universe and ourselves within them.*
> **MARK WEISER, 1996**

[Index]

A
accomplishments (contextual notification state), 77
affective technology, 28–33
alarm clocks, 74, 90–95
alpha synchrony, 79
AMBER alerts, 63
ambient awareness
  calm exercise for, 98–99
  creating, 35, 68–72
Apple Computer
  computer startup tone, 59
  designing toward simplicity, 42–45
  hapic notifications and, 64
  iPhone introduction, 47–49
artificial intelligence, 29–30
Ashley Madison, 105
attention
  continuous partial, 4
  as design consideration, 17–20
  limited bandwidth of our, 15–17
  peripheral, 21–28, 37–38, 69
attention graphs, 27–28
attention models, 25–27
audible status indicators
  about, 37
  status shouts, 64–68
  status tones, 58–61

B
bandwidth usage, 6
battery life
  calm exercise, 95–97
  designing for, 117
Beeminder web service, 81
Berners-Lee, Tim, 8
biofeedback training, 79
Brown, John Seely

on Calm Technology, vii–ix, 120, 121–126
on peripheral attention, 21, 69–70
on phases of computing, 2

C
calm interaction evaluation tools, 86–90
Calm Technology
  communication patterns. *See* communication patterns
  designing for, 1–14
  exercises in. *See* exercises (Calm Technology)
  history and future of, vii–xi, 119–126
  in organizations. *See* organizational considerations
  principles of. *See* principles of Calm Technology
captology, 78
centralized computer systems, 3
channels, dedicated, 7
cloud data storage, 11
COBOL programming language, 9
Comcast example, 7
communication patterns
  about, 53
  ambient awareness, 35, 68–72, 98–99
  contextual notifications, 37–38, 53, 73–77
  haptic alerts, 61–63, 99–100
  persuasive technology, 77–80, 78–81
  status indicators, 54–58
  status shouts, 64–68
  status tones, 58–61
Compass app (iPhone), 77

127

competition, fear of, 114
computing, waves of, 1–5
contextual notifications
    Calm Technology principles on, 37–38
    design considerations, 53
    triggering, 73–77
continuous partial attention, 4
cultural metabolization, 46–47

D

Dark Sky application, 76
decentralized computer systems, 3
"Designing Calm Technology" (Weiser and Brown), vii
designing for Calm Technology
    design considerations, 6–14
    four waves of computing, 1–5
    organizational considerations, 116–118
    principles to consider. *See* principles of Calm Technology
    privacy considerations, 105–108
desktop computing era, 1, 4–5, 18
directions, turn-by-turn, 63
Distributed Computing, 1–3, 6, 12–13

E

edge cases, , 8
electricity example, x
Email Garden installation, 73
emergency alerts, 63
emergency sirens, 67
emotional (contextual notification state), 77
environmental considerations
    calm interaction evaluation tool, 86–90
    drving cars, 37
    resource limitations, 6
    when designing objects, 16, 19–20
The Evolution of Consciousness (Ornstein), 29
exercises (Calm Technology)
    about, 85–86
    alarm clocks, 90–95
    ambient awareness, 98–99
    calmer kitchen, 96
    calm interaction evaluation tools, 86–90
    haptic alert, 99–100
    healthier eating habits, 97–98
    year-long battery, 95–97

F

false alarm example, 40–41
false positives, 67
Flux application, 76
Fogg, B.J., 78, 79
fridge for healthier eating exercise, 97–98

G

Geoloqi (company), 77
Gibson, William, 114
GlowCap cap, 79
Gold, Rich, 120
Google Chat, 21–22
Google (company), 30, 77
Google Glass, 19, 49–50, 115
Google Maps, 64
government infrastructure, 7

H

haptic alerts
    about, 38, 61–63
    calm exercise, 99–100
    car radio knobs, 57–58
    status shouts and, 65–66
hardware
    design considerations, 42
    ephemerality of, 4–5
healthier eating habits exercise, 97–98
Healthways corporation, 81
Hertling, William, 40–41
Hoffman, Guy, 33
home technology systems, 39–41, 43–44
Hue lighting system, 39, 45, 88–89
human–computer interaction
    context in, 29, 34
    design considerations, 117
    desktop computing era and, 18
    technology amplifying best of humanity, 28–33
    Xerox PARC and, vii
Hustwit, Gary, 42

I

iCloud photo storage, 11
indexing human knowledge, 29–30, 34
inner-office window example, 69–70
insulin pumps, 61
interconnected systems, 12–13
Internet of Things (IoT)
  promise of, ix
  report predictions on, 6, 11
  Ubiquitous Computing and, 2
iPhone, 47–49, 74, 77
Ive, Jony, 42

J

Jeremijenko, Natalie, , 70
Jobs, Steve, 47

K

Kay, Alan, 122
kitchen exercise, 96
kitchen timers, 74

L

lean principles, 101
Live Wire art project, 69–71, 98
local networks, 10–11
location (contextual notification state), 76
LUMOBack Sensor, 63–64

M

mainframe computing era, 1
management objections
  all legacy features must stay, 109–110
  keeping product secret until launch, 111–112
  more features are better, 108–109
  no time for user testing, 110
  what about other stakeholders, 110
McHugh, Maureen, 29
metabolic (contextual notification state), 77
Microsoft PixelSense, 111
minimalism, designing toward, 16, 95

mission critical systems, languages for, 8–10
M&M clause, 23
Multicast Backbone streaming system, 123–124

N

Naturally Intelligent Systems (McHugh), 29
Nest smoke detector, 40–41
Netflix example, 7
neurofeedback, 79
Norman, Don, 31
notifications, 37–38. *See also* communication patterns
Novak, Brennan, 50

O

Objectified (documentary), 42
object recognition, 29
OPOWER power company, 80
organizational considerations
  about, 101
  building teams, 101–104
  designing for privacy, 105–108
  product launches, 112–118
  selling to management, 108–112
Ornstein, Robert E., 29

P

Paro (robotic companion), 31–32
patterns. *See* communication patterns
perfume example, 54
peripheral attention
  Calm Technology principles on, 21–28, 37–38
  Weiser and Brown on, 21, 69–70
persuasive technology, 53, 78–81
Philips lighting system, 39, 45, 88–89
political buffers, 104
primary tasks
  affective technology and, 28
  attention graphs and, 27–28
  attention models for, 25–27
  identifying, 23–25
principles of Calm Technology
  about, 15–17
  amplifying best of humanity, 28–33

amplifying best of technology, 28–33
communicating with technology, 33–38
creating calm, 20–21
engaging peripheral attention, 21–28
informing unobtrusively, 20–21
requiring smallest possible amount of attention, 17–20
working even when failing, 38–41
privacy, designing for, 105–108
product launches, 111–118
programming languages for mission critical systems, 8–10
proximity (contextual notification state), 77

R

Rams, Dieter, 43
Rao, Venkatesh, 123
Reeks, Jim, 59
research, importance of, 114–116
robotic companions, 31–33
Rodrigues, Nick, 73
Rolling Stones (band), 123
Roomba robotic vacuum cleaner, 37, 61
Roth, David Lee, 23
Rotterdam Design Institute, 72
rule of five (teams), 102

S

Saint-Exupéry, Antoine de, 41
secondary tasks
    attention graphs, 27–28
    attention models for, 25–27
    identifying, 23–25
security breaches, 107–108
Severe Tire Damage (band), 123
simplicity, designing toward, 16, 42
Siri program, 34–35
Slack messaging software, 23–26, 117
Sleep Cycle application, 75, 75–76
smart contact lens project (Google), 77
smartwatches, 62
smoke detectors, 66
snooze buttons (alarm clocks), 74
social network space

of devices, 5
fear of competition in, 114
stakeholders, 101–103, 110
status indicators
    audible, 37, 58–61, 64–68
    design considerations, 18–19, 20–22, 35–36, 53–54
    tactile controls, 38, 57–58, 61–63, 65–66
    visual, 37, 54–56
status shouts, 64–68
status tones, 36, 58–61
Stone, Linda, 4
subscription plans for devices, 5

T

tactile controls
    about, 38, 61–63
    calm exercise, 99–100
    car radio knobs, 57–58
    status shouts and, 65–66
Taylor, Bob, viii, 123
team building in organizations, 101–104
tertiary tasks, attention models for, 25–27
testing
    teams, 103
    user, 110, 116
time (contextual notification state), 74, 76
Toyota Prius, 80
triggers and contextual notifications, 73–77
turn-by-turn directions, 63

U

Ubiquitous Computing, viii, 1–3, 121
user testing, 110, 116

V

Van Halen example, 23
Verizon example, 7
videoconferencing, 120–121
videogame controllers, 62
Virtual Aquarium, 57
VisiCalc program, 121–122
visual status indicators, 37, 54–56
voice concatenation systems, 29, 35
voice recognition systems, 33–34

W

waves of computing, 1–5
Weather-Colored Light bulb, 72
weather (contextual notification state), 76
Weiser, Mark
   on alarm clock design, 93
   on Calm Technology, vii–ix, 15, 120, 121–126
   on peripheral attention, 21, 69–70
   on phases of computing, 1–2
   on Ubiquitous Computing, viii, 1–3, 121
Withings scale, 80
Wozniak, Steve, 113

X

Xerox PARC
   Calm Technology and, vii–viii, 119–126
   Live Wire art project, , 70

About the Author

Amber Case is a cyborg anthropologist and user experience designer from Portland, Oregon. She studies the interaction between humans and computers and how our relationship with information is changing the way cultures think, act, and understand their worlds.

She is the cofounder and former CEO of Geoloqi, a location-based software company acquired by Esri in 2012. She spoke about the future of the interface for SXSW 2012's keynote address, and her TED talk, "We are all cyborgs now," has been viewed over a million times. Named one of *National Geographic*'s Emerging Explorers, she's been listed among *Inc. Magazine*'s 30 under 30 and featured among *Fast Company*'s Most Influential Women in Technology. In 2008, Case founded CyborgCamp, an unconference on the future of humans and computers.

Case is the author of *An Illustrated Dictionary of Cyborg Anthropology* and *Calm Technology* as well as numerous articles on the Web. You can follow her on Twitter *@caseorganic* and learn more at *caseorganic.com*.

Colophon

The animal on the cover of *Calm Technology* is a Sunda slow loris (*Nycticebus coucang*), an arboreal primate found throughout the tropical rainforests of Indonesia, Malaysia, Thailand, and Singapore. These solitary animals are often referred to as *malu-malu*, the Indonesian word for "shy."

The Sunda slow loris measures about 11 to 15 inches long. It has a round head with large, dark-rimmed eyes separated by a white strip of fur ending at the nose. Its thick, woolly coat is brown in color, and features a dark stripe that runs from the back of its head along its spine. It also has a vestigial tail.

The slow loris is nocturnal, sleeping on tree branches curled up in a tight ball. Its diet includes tree sap, floral nectar, and fruit. The species is at serious risk of extinction due to hunting for the exotic pet trade and habitat loss.

Many of the animals on O'Reilly covers are endangered; all of them are important to the world. To learn more about how you can help, go to *animals.oreilly.com*.

The cover image is an animal illustration by Karen Montgomery, based on an engraving from *Meyers Kleines Lexicon*. The cover fonts are URW Typewriter and Guardian Sans. The text font is Scala Regular; and the heading font is Gotham Narrow Medium.

Have it your way.

O'Reilly eBooks

- Lifetime access to the book when you buy through oreilly.com
- Provided in up to four, DRM-free file formats, for use on the devices of your choice: PDF, .epub, Kindle-compatible .mobi, and Android .apk
- Fully searchable, with copy-and-paste, and print functionality
- We also alert you when we've updated the files with corrections and additions.

oreilly.com/ebooks/

Safari Books Online

- Access the contents and quickly search over 7000 books on technology, business, and certification guides
- Learn from expert video tutorials, and explore thousands of hours of video on technology and design topics
- Download whole books or chapters in PDF format, at no extra cost, to print or read on the go
- Early access to books as they're being written
- Interact directly with authors of upcoming books
- Save up to 35% on O'Reilly print books

See the complete Safari Library at safaribooksonline.com

O'REILLY®

©2014 O'Reilly Media, Inc. O'Reilly logo is a registered trademark of O'Reilly Media, Inc. 14373